Leon.

Wishing you a speedy recovery

Midge & Abe.

TEDDY KOLLEK
Mayor of Jerusalem

Books by Naomi Shepherd

WILFRID ISRAEL
THE ZEALOUS INTRUDERS
TEDDY KOLLEK, MAYOR OF JERUSALEM

TEDDY KOLLEK
Mayor of Jerusalem

Naomi Shepherd

A Cornelia & Michael Bessie Book

HARPER & ROW, PUBLISHERS, New York
Cambridge, Philadelphia, San Francisco, Washington
London, Mexico City, São Paulo, Singapore, Sydney

For Sarah and Isaac

I should like to express my gratitude to Linda Osband
for her skilled help in the editing of this book.

This work was first published in Great Britain under the title *The Mayor and the Citadel*. "Mayor" by Yehuda Amichai, is taken from *The Selected Poetry of Yehuda Amichai*, edited and translated by Chana Bloch and Stephen Mitchell. English translation copyright © 1986 by Stephen Mitchell. Reprinted by permission of Harper & Row, Publishers.

FIRST U.S. EDITION

Library of Congress Cataloging-in-Publication Data

Shepherd, Naomi.
    Teddy Kollek, mayor of Jerusalem.
    "A Cornelia & Michael Bessie book."
    First published in Great Britain in 1987 under title:
The mayor and the citadel.
    Includes index.
    1. Kollek, Teddy, 1911–   . 2. Mayors—
Jerusalem—Biography.   3. Jerusalem—Biography.
I. Title.
DS109.86.K64S46   1988   956.94'405'0924 [B] 87–45666
ISBN 0-06-039084-0

88 89 90 91 92 HC 10 9 8 7 6 5 4 3 2 1

Mayor

It's sad to be
the mayor of Jerusalem—
it's terrible.
How can a man be mayor of such a city?
What can he do with it?
Build and build and build.

And at night the stones of the mountains crawl down
and surround the stone houses,
like wolves coming to howl at the dogs,
who have become the slaves of men.

—YEHUDA AMICHAI

Contents

Illustrations

The reception at the Citadel: Kollek greets Yegishe Derderian,
   Armenian Patriarch
Kollek with Cardinal John O'Connor of New York, spring 1987
Members of the Jerusalem Committee survey new building from a
   hilltop on their fourth visit to Jerusalem, April 1978
Kollek with Gerald Ford in the Old City bazaar
Kollek with flowers donated to a central park area by the people
   of Holland
Jews and Arabs in the Old City market
The Western (Wailing) Wall
The outer citadel
Aerial view of the Temple Mount, from the south-west (*Israeli Air
   Force*)
Inauguration of the Liberty Bell Garden, 1978
Rejoicing of the Law: observant soldiers on leave celebrate in the
   streets
Orthodox demonstrators protest against Kollek's plans for a football
   stadium in Jerusalem
The Admor of Gur
Kollek poses for an election picture tied up with rope
Kollek with Anwar Nusseibeh
The Old City: Arabs protest against Jewish rule in Jerusalem
After a knifing in an Old City alley, Eliahu Amedi lies dying, 13
   November 1986

*Unless otherwise stated, all the photographs are copyright ©
Rachamim Israeli*

Foreword

This account is based on six months' close observation of events in the city of Jerusalem between August 1986 and March 1987, and also on my own thirty-year experience of living in Jerusalem – divided and united.

I am grateful to the Mayor, Teddy Kollek, who allowed me a number of intimate glimpses of his working life. My warmest thanks, too, to all those who work with him in the Municipality of Jerusalem, for their readiness to answer my questions so patiently and in so much detail.

I am also indebted to those residents of the city, of all nationalities, political views and religious beliefs, who agreed to talk to me in the confidence that I would faithfully report their opinions and, in some cases, respect their wish for anonymity.

Jerusalem is a city whose beauty and apparent tranquillity conceal great conflict and controversy. I have scarcely touched, in this account, on the history of the conflict, but rather tried to examine its results in terms of the daily life of the city over the past twenty years, and its effect on the work of the extraordinary Mayor who has dominated the city throughout this time.

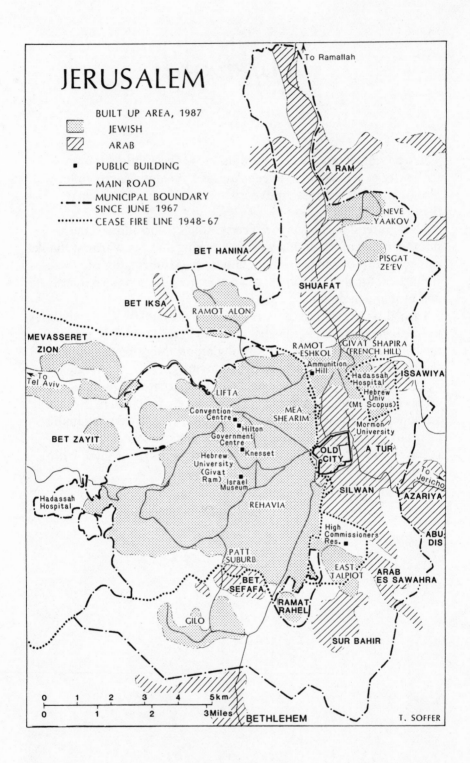

JERUSALEM

BUILT UP AREA, 1987
- JEWISH
- ARAB

■ PUBLIC BUILDING
— MAIN ROAD
▬·▬· MUNICIPAL BOUNDARY
SINCE JUNE 1967
·········· CEASE FIRE LINE 1948-67

↑ To Ramallah

A RAM

NEVE YAAKOV

BET HANINA

PISGAT ZE'EV

BET IKSA

RAMOT ALON

SHUAFAT

MEVASSERET ZION

← To Tel Aviv

RAMOT ESHKOL

GIVAT SHAPIRA (FRENCH HILL)

Ammunition Hill ■

ISSAWIYA

Hadassah Hospital ■

LIFTA

Hebrew Univ (Mt Scopus)

Convention Centre ■

MEA SHEARIM

Mormon University

■ Hilton
Government Centre ■

■ Knesset

OLD CITY

A TUR

BET ZAYIT

Hebrew University (Givat Ram)

■ Israel Museum

SILWAN

→ To Jericho

AZARIYA

Hadassah Hospital ■

REHAVIA

ABU DIS

High Commissioners Res. ■

PATT SUBURB

EAST TALPIOT

ARAB ES SAWAHRA

BET SEFAFA

RAMAT RAHEL

GILO

SUR BAHIR

0   1   2   3   4   5km
0   1   2   3Miles

BETHLEHEM

T. SOFFER

CENTRAL JERUSALEM, 1987

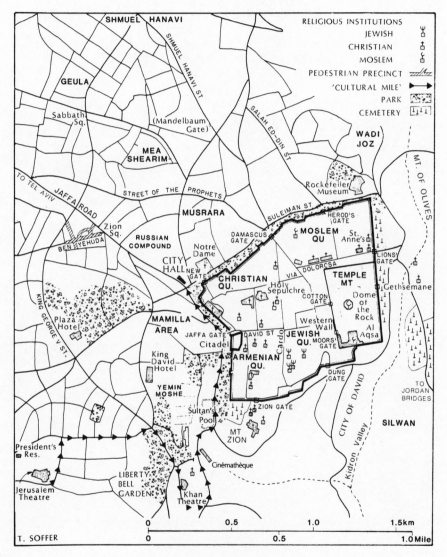

RELIGIOUS INSTITUTIONS
JEWISH
CHRISTIAN
MOSLEM
PEDESTRIAN PRECINCT
'CULTURAL MILE'
PARK
CEMETERY

SHMUEL HANAVI

SHMUEL HANAVI ST

GEULA

Sabbath Sq.

(Mandelbaum Gate)

MEA SHEARIM

SALAH ED-DIN ST

WADI JOZ

MT. OF OLIVES

TO TEL AVIV

JAFFA ROAD

STREET OF THE PROPHETS

Rockefeller Museum

Zion Sq.

MUSRARA

SULEIMAN ST

HEROD'S GATE

RUSSIAN COMPOUND

BEN YEHUDA

Notre Dame

DAMASCUS GATE

MOSLEM QU

St. Anne's

LIONS' GATE

CITY HALL

NEW GATE

CHRISTIAN QU.

VIA DOLOROSA

Gethsemane

KING GEORGE V ST.

Plaza Hotel

MAMILLA AREA

Holy Sepulchre

COTTON GATE

TEMPLE MT

Dome of the Rock

Al Aqsa

JAFFA GATE

Citadel

DAVID ST

Cardo

JEWISH QU.

Western Wall

MOORS' GATE

King David Hotel

ARMENIAN QU.

YEMIN MOSHE

Sultan's Pool

ZION GATE

DUNG GATE

CITY OF DAVID

TO JORDAN BRIDGES

President's Res.

MT ZION

SILWAN

Jerusalem Theatre

LIBERTY BELL GARDEN

Cinémathèque

Khan Theatre

Kidron Valley

| 0 | | 0.5 | | 1.0 | | 1.5km |

| 0 | | | 0.5 | | | 1.0 Mile |

T. SOFFER

1

The View from the Citadel

TWICE A YEAR, on Israel's Independence Day and the Jewish Feast of Tabernacles, the Mayor of Jerusalem, Teddy Kollek, holds an official reception at the Citadel. A Herodian ruin rebuilt by the Crusaders and the Turks, the Citadel was for centuries a garrison at Jerusalem's most vulnerable angle, at the north-west corner of the Old City walls. In the political sense, this is still true. Here west Jerusalem meets east, and Israel's claim to the city in its entirety has never been fully recognized by the outside world. The Citadel and the Mayor are still embattled.

To the outside world, Kollek appears as the colossus of Jerusalem, with one foot planted on its western, one on its eastern side since the reunification of the city by military conquest on 7 June 1967, and the introduction of Israeli law there on 27 June. This year, the anniversary of the latter date coincided, in the Hebrew calendar, with Kollek's seventy-sixth birthday.

Kollek's name is associated with Israel's rule of the city 'sacred to three religions' and it is his policies, it is widely believed, which have staved off conflict between the Jewish majority and Arab minority there during the past twenty years. Kollek is also the man who has probably done most in this century to remind the West of its historic links with Jerusalem and to enlist its support – chiefly within the Jewish diaspora but also in non-Jewish circles in Europe and America – for the city's restoration and development. He stands for both the conservation of the monumental Old City and the expansion of the new – to both of which he has devoted his prodigious energies.

Within Jerusalem, Kollek is a figure of solidity and dependability, the man who, having defeated all rivals, has governed Jerusalem for over twenty-one years. He is also Jerusalem's most peripatetic mayor, continually campaigning abroad on the city's behalf and, within the city, constantly on the move with visiting politicians, benefactors and pilgrims. He is very conscious of the sensitivity of Jerusalem's international status and its uniqueness; together with Levi Eshkol, Israel's Prime Minister in 1967, Kollek opposed 'twinning' the city with New York – a suggestion supported by Menachem Begin, the right-wing leader, as New York appeared to him to be the great city of Jewish sanctuary.

While the parks, museums, concert halls and community centres of the new Jerusalem bear plaques attesting to the generosity of men and women whom he himself has recruited, not a single project bears Kollek's name. It was only in March 1987, following a period of unprecedented challenge to his leadership, that a group of his supporters organized the planting of a grove of saplings on a hillside overlooking the Old City from the south-west, dedicated to Kollek. These, according to the programme, are almond, olive and pistachio trees, and rosemary bushes. It is eventually intended that this grove will be extended to include pine trees, thus, say his admirers, symbolizing Kollek's often declared views of Jerusalem as a 'pluralist' city shared between Jews, Moslems and Christians.

The parallel could be carried further. Pines are favoured by the Israeli forestry commission because they are fast growing, need relatively little care and within a decade change the appearance of the landscape, while the olive, almond and other fruit trees which also grow on the Jerusalem hillsides need much attention and care – usually from the local Arab villagers – if they are to produce fruit regularly. Each species needs its own space, and each will grow separately, and apart, at a different pace. Hence the challenge of governing Jerusalem.

A grey stone fortress with a disused mosque and minaret at its southern end, the Citadel stands where the modern city touches the old. Nearby, the Jaffa Road leads west towards the sea, only thirty miles away in the plain. The road to Hebron which passes just beneath the walls of the Citadel leads south, skirting the desert, to the city of Abraham, common ancestor to Jews and Moslems. For this reason, the medieval entrance to the Old City just beside the Citadel is known not only as the Jaffa Gate, but to Arabs as the Gate of the Friend, and an Arabic inscription high on the wall reads: 'There is no God but Allah, and Ibrahim is his Friend.' All the ancient gates, the streets, the shrines, even the city itself have two different names at least, each name with its own history and its particular claim.

Over the past century four different rulers have held the Citadel: Turkish, British, Jordanian and Israeli. In 1898 the Turkish Sultan breached the low wall between the Jaffa Gate and the Citadel to let the German Kaiser ride in state into the city. General Allenby entered Jerusalem in 1917 on foot and addressed the populace from the main entrance to the Citadel, inside the walls. In 1948 the Jordanians placed sandbags on the fortifications, and the road to Hebron was impassable; it led through no man's land after the division of the city. Now a Jewish mayor holds his celebrations here – not inside the Citadel, but on a platform just outside the walls. To reach the platform guests must make their way through the heavy traffic passing to and from the centre of the city. Invitations warn them to dress warmly. Even on an afternoon in autumn, the platform is first exposed to the afternoon sun, and then to the sudden chill of the Jerusalem evening – a reminder of the nearness of the desert, like the ochre stains on the limestone walls from sand carried here by a storm in Sinai a hundred and thirty years ago.

Kollek, a short man with a powerful head and shoulders and a mane of grey hair, stands beneath the only tree near the roadside, shaking hundreds of hands and scanning faces. Among the Jewish guests are lawyers wealthy enough to take time off from their offices; community workers; a Russian immigrant in a cloth cap who complains to everyone that he knows no one at the party; and philanthropists in town to unveil dedication plaques. Among the foreigners are the consular corps in their regimental suits and ties, and the Eastern church hierarchy, each with its distinctive headdress and formal robes. Among the Arab guests are the village *mukhtars* in their checked *keffiyot*, and the municipal officials in their brown suits and knitted waistcoats. The reception is less a Jewish social event than a barometer of the Mayor's relations with the consuls, the churches and the Arabs of the city.

There is no real security check at the ramp leading to the platform: Kollek always says he does not believe in it. But a nervous municipal official in a peaked cap, carrying a walkie-talkie, rummages inside the Tabernacle booth, which is made of coloured sheets, decorated with party ribbons and covered with branches, and a police wagon is parked at the Jaffa Gate. The municipal guard feels among the stacks of soft drink cartons and then, reassured, helps himself to a piece of sliced honey cake from a brass tray carried past by a municipal charlady.

Former Israeli mayors held their annual receptions at the Rose Garden, a secluded, pine-shaded park to the west of the city. After the Israeli victory in the Six Day War, Kollek chose the Citadel, which stands astride what was for nineteen years the ceasefire line and effective frontier between Israel and Jordan, Jews and Arabs. This is the real centre of the city, with all its conflicts and problems, unlike the President's mansion to the west of town, where more elegant and formal receptions are held at the same times of year.

The reception is outside the walls for a reason. When the Mayor first sent out his invitations, the consular corps, which continued to maintain the fiction of a 'Jordanian' east and an 'Israeli' west of the city, refused to attend. They accepted only when it was explained that the platform where the reception would be held was in former no man's land. The consuls are still in Jerusalem as envoys to a *corpus separatum*, as the city was to become under the 1947 United Nations plan for the partition of Palestine. So is the Apostolic Delegate, the Vatican envoy, who has no diplomatic relations with the State of Israel. The Arabs of the city do not recognize Israeli sovereignty; and very few of those present at Tabernacles will come on Independence Day.

So the Mayor and his Jewish guests are in the reunified capital of the State of Israel; the consuls are in no man's land between Israel and Jordan; the Arabs are in occupied Palestine under foreign rule; and the Christian clergy are in a city of shrines and churches, Holy Places in which their several rights are laid down in a document issued over a hundred years ago by a Turkish sultan. This code is interpreted by the Mayor's team: the External Affairs Advisor from the Ministry of Foreign Affairs, the Christian Affairs Advisor and the Arab Affairs Advisor – a retinue similar to that of a cabinet minister. The British Consul warns his wife not to wander beyond the Citadel entrance for reasons of protocol; the American benefactors admire the view.

The Citadel overlooks a long valley sloping from the city centre to the desert hills just visible to the south. From the horizon, to the west, stretches part of Kollek's 'Cultural Mile': parks with spinning sprinklers, the red-tiled roofs of town houses for the privileged, a nineteenth-century Jewish almshouse converted into a guesthouse for distinguished visitors. Due south, in the Vale of Gehenna, where the children of biblical legend were sacrificed to Moloch, is the café terrace of the Cinémathèque, where Kurosawa and Monty Python films are showing in a double bill, and a music school where Jewish and Arab children are practising on recorders and drums. Immediately below the walls of the Old City is the Sultan's Pool, a grassy basin which a hundred years ago was a cattle market. Now it is renamed for the benefactors from New York, landscaped and fitted with a mobile auditorium occupied on summer nights by Verdi, Judy Collins, Dire Straits, Sadler's Wells. Only a few days before the reception, fifteen hundred American Jewish fund-raisers filed into the Sultan's Pool for a sound-and-light display, which included the floodlighting of a plaster Statue of Liberty on the walls beside the Citadel. After a ceremony celebrating American Jews' 'equal contribution' to the State of Israel, Kollek was presented with a portrait of Ben Gurion. 'A little bit of *schmaltz*, but it's all true,' was Kollek's comment on the display, while young Israelis at the gate distributed handouts whose message ended: 'Charity No! Immigration Yes!'

Nearer the city centre stretches a thirty-acre field of asphalt and rubble, edged by roofless houses with gaping window frames. This is not just the result of Jerusalem's wars, as some of the guests surmise. The site was recently levelled for the most grandiose project yet proposed for the city: a commercial centre designed years ago to link Jewish and Arab Jerusalem, but delayed for nearly two decades by planners' quarrels, city politics and the perennial lack of funds.

The greening of the valley and the 'Cultural Mile' are the most visible signs of Kollek's efforts to make Jerusalem into what he calls a 'world city' (derivation: *Welstadt*), with all the cultural and recreational facilities of a Western capital. The field of asphalt and rubble signals his more controversial role as a city administrator. But it is the attendances, and the absences, at the Citadel reception which indicate his most important role: as referee of the barely dormant conflicts in the city.

As far as Kollek and the consuls are concerned, the Tabernacles reception takes place during a lull in hostilities. The recently arrived American consul, Morris Draper, is an old acquaintance: Philip Habib's assistant in negotiations during the Lebanon War. But Kollek's relations with the smaller fry have always been problematic. When the consuls failed to appear at a reception he gave in 1969,

Kollek billed them all for city taxes – from which they are officially exempt. If they did not recognize him, he explained to pained Israeli officials, he would not recognize them. This was only one in a long series of 'misunderstandings'.

Today the Common Market consuls are all smiles, but within a few weeks there is trouble. Invited to the City Hall to meet the new Prime Minister, Yitzhak Shamir, they inform Kollek's Foreign Affairs Advisor at the last moment that they cannot attend 'lest they compromise their position on Jerusalem'. Enraged, Kollek fires off a letter, in which he says: 'We in Jerusalem are trying to promote harmony and understanding rather than discord, and I consider actions such as yours both destructive and detrimental to these aims.'

At the reception, the balance of power between the Jerusalem churches is more obvious than usual. The Greek Orthodox contingent, in heavily jewelled regalia, includes visiting bishops from Romania and Poland, and puts the Latins (Catholics) in the shade. The Orthodox are holding a conference in the city to celebrate the sixteen-hundredth anniversary of the entrance into Jerusalem of Cyril, first Greek bishop of Jerusalem. This is a signal to the Catholics, celebrating the year of Peace in Rome and Assisi, that the Eastern Church has a longer pedigree in the Holy Land than its Western rival.

The Armenian and Syrian Orthodox clergy are present and correct, but not on speaking terms. The repair of one section of the great Rotunda of the Holy Sepulchre, under scaffolding for thirty years, is still incomplete because of their disputes: the right to repair is part of the rights of possession. The Copts and the Ethiopians also keep apart. The Ethiopians have occupied a rooftop of the Holy Sepulchre ever since the Copts invaded *their* property, as they claim, when all the Ethiopian clergy died of the plague in 1838. The Copts, for their part, are still smarting because, during the 1960s – when Israel was the enemy of Egypt, the Copts' protectors – the Israeli government upheld the Ethiopian seizure of a nearby passageway.

There is a splendid display of Eastern ecclesiastical robes and Western dogcollars. But the fur *streimels* and silk caftans of the orthodox rabbis are missing. The ultra-orthodox Jews and Kollek exchange no compliments these days, and Kollek is seen more frequently at church ceremonies than in their company. In a recent interview he said that he had been invited into an ultra-orthodox *yeshiva* in Jerusalem only once: to fill sandbags during the Six Day War.

The Moslem Mufti and his colleagues, sworn enemies of Israel, are not invited; the heads of the Wakf, the Moslem Trust which administers religious property, who have necessary dealings with the city, are invited but do not attend. The Arabs present are the clan leaders of city districts and villages, and the municipal employees: teachers in government schools, clerks, sanitation and gardening contractors. The head of the East Jerusalem Chamber of Commerce is not present, but there are a few businessmen and shopkeepers, the bolder of whom try to raise tax problems with Kollek or lobby for permits with his Advisor. Their presence, like that of the Christians, is registered and ticked off later on a list. The reception, informal though it looks, is in reality a very delicate exercise in municipal relations.

As the man who has presided for two decades over the threefold expansion of a famous city, Teddy Kollek is often compared with men like Baron Haussmann, Prefect of the Seine and rebuilder of Paris during the Second Empire; or with Robert Moses, the powerful Parks Commissioner of New York. Both Haussmann and Moses changed the faces of their cities. But Kollek has as little in common with these men as Jerusalem has with Paris or New York.

Haussmann and Moses both drew on the immense wealth of their cities. Haussmann mortgaged Paris to the hilt, borrowed directly from the public and from the renegade Crédit Mobilier. Moses raised the money to build his highways and bridges by issuing bonds in the names of the public authorities he controlled, and so made himself independent of the governor, state legislature and mayor of the city. Both men cut huge swathes through the poorer districts of their cities and turned thousands out of their homes. Haussmann had the power of Louis Napoleon behind him and Moses bent the city's municipal leaders to his will.

Jerusalem is a poor city in a small country, its only dowry its historical reputation and natural beauty. Kollek's own statutory powers are slight: those of an official dependent on city taxes and government handouts for his budget, and with very little authority to carry out projects on his own. It is the Israeli government, not Kollek, which has built the enormous suburbs and the linking highways which now girdle the city.

Like Haussmann, Kollek repaired the city's drains; and like Moses, he laid out parks for the people. But his power comes from a different source, perhaps more remarkable than that of either of those men. The hundreds of millions of dollars that Kollek has raised for the city, almost single-handed, have come from abroad, in the form of tax-free gifts as a tribute to the city and, to a great extent, to the abilities of the man himself.

Jerusalem was, until a few decades ago, a small town, half rural, half urban. The mandatory government and Israel made it into an administrative centre — first for Palestine, then for the Jewish state. But only since 1967 has the city played a role in world politics, and Kollek, an able government official turned city impresario, a part in international affairs. There is a price for such prominence. Jerusalem now lies on the fault line of the Arab–Israel conflict; it is 'the last item on the agenda', the subject of the most difficult of all the territorial disputes between Israel and the Arab states. Kollek, 'the world's most famous mayor', is the city's troubleshooter.

The move from the Rose Garden to the Citadel, from Jerusalem as a backwater to Jerusalem resurgent, meant the difference between running a city with a political consensus and coping with a large minority deeply hostile to Israeli rule. It meant linking a town with standardized modern services to one including the only surviving medieval city in the Middle East, and to the farming villages on the outskirts. It meant taking over responsibility for the protection of the Christian Holy Places and the church institutions, and the encouragement of pilgrimage. All this had to take place under the critical scrutiny of a distinctly unfriendly United Nations. One clear reminder of this hostility is the continued presence of the UN Truce Supervisory Commission maintaining an 'armistice agreement' which ended in 1967. Another is the constant warfare, by UNESCO, on Israeli archaeological and restoration work in the city.

When Israel extended its legal powers to Arab Jerusalem and declared the city to be united, it did so in the name of ancient history and millennial religious aspirations. But Jerusalem was united only in the physical sense. For the first time since the establishment of the state, Israelis now encountered, face to face, in their capital, a population which had no intention of repeating the mistakes of an earlier generation of refugees and leaving their homes to the Jews. East Jerusalem, in comparison with the Jewish west, was neglected. King Hussein of Jordan had invested most of his financial resources on the east bank of the river and had chosen Amman for his capital. Jerusalem remained a centre of Palestinian nationalism, where Hussein's grandfather, Abdullah, had been assassinated in 1952, and its élite was divided between those who supported the Jordanian government and those who wanted Palestinian independence. All, however, were equally opposed to Israeli rule.

Moreover, Jerusalem is the one place where the Arab–Israel conflict focusses on religious as well as nationalist issues, threatening to pit the entire Moslem world against the Jewish state.

The Jews' Temple Mount, at the heart of the Old City, is the Moslems' Noble Sanctuary. The site of the First and Second Temples is also the third most sacred site in Islam after Mecca and Medina. The western wall of the Sanctuary is also the Western (Wailing) Wall of the Jews. The Al Aqsa mosque, literally a stone's throw from the Western Wall, is the rallying point for Arab political demonstrations in the city.

Controlling Christian Jerusalem means far more than ensuring freedom of access and worship in the Christian Holy Places. It involves the well-being of entire communities, with their senior hierarchy of foreigners, and their parish priests and lay members, most of whom are Christian Arabs, Jordanian citizens with ties in the surrounding Arab states. Any mishap in their treatment would make further trouble for Israel in the international arena.

The Latin church looks for its leadership to the Vatican, with the prestige and influence it wields in Europe (particularly in Italy and France) and elsewhere in the Catholic world. The older established Greek Orthodox church deals with Israel more directly, and is also more dependent on Israel's goodwill. But while Israel fears to alienate the Vatican, in the context of Western politics, it also wishes the Greek Orthodox church, with its millions of adherents in Eastern Europe, to remain content and co-operative. It does not make matters easier for Israel that the two great churches are traditionally rivals in Jerusalem.

The Armenian church, with its titular head in Soviet Armenia, provides the shifting balance between the Latins and the Greeks, siding with the first on the religious issues in the city (since the Greeks try continually to enlarge their territory) and with the second on political questions. All the churches seek a new statutory definition of privilege, which would make them more independent of Israel, or indeed of whatever government rules Jerusalem.

So maintaining Israeli rule over Jerusalem with a minimum of friction depends on a very discreet interpretation of sovereign rights. The Temple Mount, or Sanctuary, is under the administration of the Moslem Wakf, which controls all but one of the entrance gates to the precinct and decides the hours during which it is open to the public. Traditionally, rabbis have banned access to the site of the Temple until the arrival of the Messiah. Thus, immediately after the Six Day War, the Israeli government, basing its decision on a passage in Maimonides, ruled that the Jews may not pray there. Tens of administrative compromises have been made in the eastern part of the city to accommodate Moslem and Christian sensibilities and to avoid needless conflict with the Arab population. And Kollek, now in his fifth term as mayor of the reunified city, defines Jerusalem, to those who visit it as a multi-ethnic, multi-religious city in which each group is free to lead its own separate life.

The Jerusalem municipality is still housed in the old, British-built premises not far from the Citadel, with a plaque commemorating its inauguration in 1930 by the British District Commissioner in the presence of Mayor Ragueb Bey Nashashibi, of one of the most famous Palestinian Arab families. There is a shabby, relaxed air to the place. The porters barely challenge visitors ('Where to? Mayor's Office? Know the way?'), who have the choice of walking up three flights of stairs or squeezing into a temperamental three-man lift. Entrance to the Mayor's presence is through a windowless waiting-room in which an old mahogany cabinet displays gifts from fellow mayors and city benefactors: from the inevitable pewter beer mugs to carved bears and lions (cartoonists compare Kollek to both).

Kollek's door stands open during most meetings, so that he can call to his 'girls' in the neighbouring office. He has no intercom and his air conditioning was put in only last year.

In one corner of the big, comfortable office is a pyramid of stuffed teddy bears. Nothing could be more incongruous than this reminder of the name by which everyone calls him. Despite lapses into boyish good humour, and the devastating charm he lavishes on favoured visitors (donors, VIPs) and the man in the street, Kollek is not a man to encourage intimacy. Anyone who wants to work with him has to accept his sudden and destructive rages, his impatience with routine detail and his dislike of criticism. Yet in his city departments, there can be found many of the ablest men and women ever to work in these ill-paid, demanding local government jobs.

Kollek has no discernible life outside his passion for the city. His working hours run from dawn to near midnight and he finds little time to be with family. His wife, Tamar, a dedicated worker for voluntary causes, is reputedly a stabilizing influence in his life. He keeps – for so public a personality – a remarkably private atmosphere around his own family affairs.

He speaks of Jerusalem almost as if it were a separate entity from the rest of the country – which in a sense it is. He refers to those who abandon the city as other Israelis speak of those who leave the country. But he has never defined in so many words the nature of his attachment to the city. He was born in Nagyvaszony, a small village near Budapest, not in Jerusalem, where he has lived since 1952, seventeen years after he arrived in the country from Vienna, the city of his youth. Of his first visit in 1935 he was to write, 'I remember being impressed by [Jerusalem] as pleasant but pretty dull.' Asked to name a favourite walk, or occupation, he says: 'Whatever I'm doing at the moment'. His current projects are the massive promenade which now straddles the hillside overlooking the city from the south-west, and the recently opened Ben Yehuda pedestrian precinct at the centre of the western business area.

Some of those who know him say that Jerusalem gives him power; some that his attachment to the city is a sensual one; some that he misses 'its essential poetry'. His political rivals say he is a 'salesman of an outstanding property'. A Jewish politician says that he is, where Jerusalem is concerned, the supreme pragmatist; a Christian church-man says that Kollek has a vision for Jerusalem as a pluralist city but that it is 'quite unrealistic'. Most agree that he is a better politician than an administrator; many Israeli politicians envy Kollek his success in running Jerusalem and his international fame. The only Jerusalem Arab whose abilities Kollek respected, the late Anwar Nusseibeh, said that he would have hated to have run against Kollek at elections. Kollek himself argues that he is an administrator, not a politician. That is a politician's observation. Kollek may not be a party politician in the Israeli mould, but in every other sense he is the politician absolute.

Visiting statesmen, prime ministers, churchmen, envoys on special missions to the Israeli government, spend hours closeted with Kollek. Within a few weeks, during the autumn and winter of 1986/7, he had talks with Max Kampelman, President Reagan's man at the arms talks, who dropped off on his way back from Geneva to brief the government; Richard Shifter, American Under-Secretary of State for Human Rights; Edward Kennedy (the Kennedys and the Rockefellers are people Kollek terms 'old friends'); Cardinal John O'Connor of New York, who disappointed the waiting priests at Nazareth but not the Mayor of Jerusalem; and Bob Hawke, the Australian Prime Minister.

Apart from political and ecclesiastical visitors, there is a non-stop cavalcade of musicians and actors whose arrival delights Kollek not only because they help promote tourism and discourage the fear of terrorists, but also because the Mayor has a very low boredom threshold. In the autumn there was Isaac Stern, who preferred the admirers in the King David Hotel foyer to the quiet anonymity of Kollek's guesthouse; and Jack Lemmon, on a long day's journey to Jerusalem, for whom Kollek waited a long hour at the Cinémathèque. The Mayor never loses a chance to pose his celebrities, political or not, against the background of his rejuvenated city. It might be Jimmy Carter, jogging doggedly along the reconstructed Ramparts Walk overlooking the Old City; or Elizabeth Taylor and Richard Burton reading the Book of Ruth and *Under Milk Wood* at the Jerusalem Theatre; or Zubin Mehta conducting Tchaikovsky's 1812 overture at the Sultan's Pool, with fireworks blazing over the Old City walls and the cannon part played by the Ottoman museum piece, which more usually announces the fast of Ramadan. Or Artur Rubinstein, whose ashes are now buried in a forest overlooking the western approaches to the city, and whose widow came to Jerusalem, in the autumn of 1986, to revisit the site with Kollek.

The ultimate purpose of all Kollek's efforts is to win legitimacy for Israeli rule in the city. He has not been able to change diplomatic facts, and recalls only one small victory over the odds: in 1981, in an all-night session, he managed to persuade the then American Secretary of State, Alexander Haig, that the two American consulates should hold one Fourth of July celebration for Jews and Arabs together.

Nor has Kollek any illusion about the fragility of what he has achieved. When he was asked to 'sum up his message' for a journalist in 1985, he answered: 'That tolerance here still has very shallow roots', an expression he often repeats. Tolerance in Jerusalem has two meanings, in its political sense, for Kollek: tolerance by Jews, of the Arab presence; and tolerance, by Arabs, of Israeli rule. In the early years after 1967 he appeared more afraid of the threat from the outside world; then, he wanted everything done at once – building, planting, legislating – because in two, three, five years, 'Jerusalem is going to be on the negotiating table'. Sometimes he has persuaded foreign leaders and officials to tour the eastern part of the city with him, in accordance with the fiction that the mayor of Jerusalem is a non-political figure. And again, sometimes not. When American Treasury Secretary Michael Blumenthal refused to visit east Jerusalem on an official visit in 1977, Kollek refused to meet him. Kollek's distinguished political guests almost invariably go on to hold talks with Palestinian leaders in east Jerusalem. Catholic spokesmen discouraged Cardinal O'Connor from touring Jerusalem in Kollek's company because 'the correct escort should be a priest and not a secular mayor of another faith [*sic*]'.

The Jordanians were not recognized internationally as rulers of east Jerusalem by right; like Israel, they held half the city as the result of military conquest. Yet even according to the Camp David agreements of 1978, a return to the 1967 *status quo ante* in Jerusalem is regarded by the Americans as a necessary preliminary to some kind of accommodation in the city between Israel and Jordan, in consultation with the Palestinian leadership. In the municipality, while Kollek tends to resent the official visitors' meetings with the notables in east Jerusalem as a slight to Israel's status, there are others who argue that the visitors realize during the meetings themselves how little authority the Palestinian spokesmen enjoy, even within their own community.

But what Kollek has achieved in the diplomatic sense is the informal consensus, among Israel's friends, that the city should not be physically redivided. Even Egyptian President Sadat, on his unique visit to Jerusalem in 1977 (the present leader, Hosni Mubarak, will not visit the city), said that he objected to the idea of redivision, and proposed twin Jordanian and Israeli sovereignty. He also offered Kollek financial help for the restoration of the Al Aqsa mosque, which had been damaged in a fire set off by a deranged Australian tourist in 1969. It was typical of Kollek that he had a press release prepared instantly and handed it over to Walter Cronkite, whom he happened to meet in the lift of the King David Hotel, a few minutes later.

How does Kollek get his message across? He wastes little time on formalities and small talk. The Mayor makes his own protocol and thinks nothing of placing a hand on the shoulder of royalty, offering visitors' books to men before women, and interrupting secretaries of state in mid-sentence. He is disconcertingly willing to talk about the most sensitive aspects of Israeli rule in Jerusalem in a way that often makes the professional Israeli diplomat's hair stand on end. But he also slowly, and painstakingly, builds up relationships with politicians, officials, influential friends abroad so that a word, a cable, a message in the right place, during a crisis, will have the effect he wants.

Kollek's persuasive skills are all the more surprising in that he is not naturally an eloquent man, and his formal education never went beyond that of the Viennese *gymnasium*. He has, quite literally, no language of his own. He hardly uses his mother tongue. Hebrew, for Kollek, as for so many Israeli politicians of his generation who were not born in the country, is a blunt instrument. He is most fluent in English, which he speaks with a pronounced German accent and decorates with outdated idioms. The search for the right word makes some people long-winded: not so Kollek, who talks rapidly, with a murmur in between phrases. Foreign listeners appreciate the lack of rhetoric standard to almost every other Israeli politician. If Kollek has a problem in communication, it is that he has been telling people what to think about Jerusalem for so long that his briefings are by now a kind of shorthand.

On the walls of his office he has, among other copies of ancient maps, one of the famous clover-leaf drawings by the German Heinrich

Buenting, showing Jerusalem at the centre of three continents: 'Most burgomasters believe their city is the centre of the world. . . . I'm the only one who can prove it.' He uses two adjoining photographs to introduce Jerusalem to those who know little about the city's recent history: one shows the dividing walls, put up at the most dangerous sectors of the frontier, falling to the sappers' charges immediately after the 1967 war; the other is of the Berlin Wall: 'That's what we don't want to go back to.' It is typical of Kollek that he uses a familiar European symbol to make his point.

When he addresses a group from the European Parliament, he gives them a rough rundown on the city without at any point making speeches about the 'eternal capital of the Jewish people'. Instead, he refers to the Jordanians as 'the sub-tenants who neglected the city'. When he took over east Jerusalem, he tells them, it was a place where 'no one paid taxes and no one got services'. He describes his own role in the city as rather like that of a master plumber who installed running water, put down drains and cleared out the garbage. More subtly, he pictures Jerusalem as a city where, by tradition, each community lives apart and separate from the others – Jews, Arabs and the multiple Christian churches – equal but different. 'The Greek Orthodox have been here from the word go, and the Armenians are a separate community with their own quarter, and there are the Ethiopians and the Copts and the Assyrians – they all settled here during the first centuries after Christ. The Catholics are relative late-comers [when the audience is solidly Protestant, Kollek calls the Catholics 'Johnnies-come-lately' – a favourite term; when the audience is a wider one, it is the Protestants who are the 'Johnnies'] and the Protestants were the last to arrive.'

If guests from other 'multi-ethnic' cities abroad ask about the integration of the various communities through housing and education projects, Kollek explains to them firmly that, in Jerusalem, integration of that kind is inappropriate. Each community wants its children educated in its own tradition, its own language, and to observe its own customs, 'to smell the smell of its own cooking'. This is a persuasive argument, but it does not touch on the most fundamental problem of the city: that Jerusalem is divided between two politically opposed groups – Jewish and Arab, Israeli and Palestinian. The Christian community is a small minority of fourteen thousand in a city of nearly half a million, and the Israeli nightmare is a possible alliance against Israel between Moslem and Christian leaders.

Kollek is very frank about the hostility of Jerusalem's Arabs to Israel. 'We don't expect them to acknowledge our help in public,' he explains. 'Unfortunately, they're not represented on the City Council; no Arab could serve on an Israeli organization without risking his life. Political assassination is still a factor in this part of the world.' But many Arab residents of the city, he adds, vote for his faction at the municipal elections. Not because they like him, he explains, but because they want their rights as citizens protected.

Kollek spends much of his time touring the city with important guests and showing them the parks, the reconstruction work in the Old City, the new promenades and the Israeli-sponsored Sheikh Jarrah Health Centre, which caters for some forty thousand Arabs in the city. Kollek is an old-style Zionist who believes that Israel's claim to the city is best supported not by what is said, but by what is done for the people who live there; i.e., that economic development can compensate for and, in the end, outweigh the Arab demand for political self-determination. Since anyone who tours the city properly can see for himself that many Arab districts and villages look neglected and shabby compared with the Jewish suburbs. Kollek does not attempt to explain this just in terms of the social and economic structure of the Arab sector, and the state of the eastern city prior to 1967. He admits that he has not been able to do what he wished for the Arabs, particularly where housing and schools are concerned, but, he explains, 'it's a costly business to bring services in the Arab districts up to our level, and government help is necessary'.

Here the Mayor's famous temper starts flickering. The municipality has few powers, he explains. Israel has inherited the centralized system of local government established under the British mandate. The mayor has no authority; he is unable even to frame a by-law without consent from a government office, or to levy taxes beyond the basic rates and licensing fees for commercial premises.

'The support we get from the government barely pays for the flags we hang out on national holidays,' Kollek tells the visitors. Or, 'I feel when I talk to the government that I'm talking to the commissars'; or, 'I feel as if I were still living under a colonial regime.' His description of himself as a browbeaten clerk is so much at odds with the image of power and confidence he projects that such remarks provoke amusement rather than sympathy, and sometimes raised eyebrows. But the message comes across clearly: the Mayor of Jerusalem is, in all respects, above politics, and if the tolerant, liberal policies he represents sometimes go wrong, much of the responsibility is that of the government.

'My greatest disappointment', says Kollek, 'is that I haven't been able to change the status of the city. I've been trying for years to persuade the government to grant Jerusalem special status as a capital city, but they wouldn't move. It's my greatest failure.'

The Mayor has a long list of grudges against the government. Jerusalem is the legal capital of Israel, with the Knesset, the Supreme Court of Justice and the government ministries – except for the Defence Ministry and the army headquarters, which are in Tel Aviv. But the government maintains many annexes in Tel Aviv, where the party political headquarters, the big Histadrut Labour Federation and other major organizations are also to be found. There have been no government inducements to bring major newspapers or state theatres from Tel Aviv to the capital, and Kollek has been struggling for years for a special development budget.

Far more serious is the fact that the Mayor of Jerusalem cannot even decide policy inside the city without reference to one or another government ministry. Jerusalem has no municipal lands and cannot build its own housing. State land (including all that in east Jerusalem) belongs to the powerful Israel Lands Authority, which (since there is hardly any inherited property in the young state) controls virtually all the land reserves in the country. The Ministry of Housing has the monopoly of public housing schemes. City planners must refer each and every project to the Ministry of the Interior's District Planning Committee, on which the city has only four out of fifteen members. In education, welfare and transport, the city is dependent on government policy and government funds to supplement its budget. Municipal licensing authorities which inspect hotels and restaurants are duplicated by teams from the Ministries of Tourism and Health. The Mayor cannot license a busker in a pedestrian precinct without referring the decision to the Ministry of Justice, or put up a stop sign at a crossroads without the permission of the Ministry of Transport.

All this began with a municipal ordinance adopted by the mandatory government in 1934 which has never been revoked. The ministries which control the fate of Jerusalem are in the hands of politicians whose decisions reflect Israel's coalition policies. The upper echelons of the civil service are highly politicized. The Housing Ministry is at present a right-wing stronghold run by men who believe that building homes for Arabs will encourage them to outnumber the Jews. The Ministry of Religious Affairs dictates policy where Jerusalem's greatest Jewish monument, the Western (Wailing) Wall, is concerned, and for years has blocked various plans for the development of the vast square facing it; its aesthetic views do not coincide with those of the city's planners and environmentalists. The Interior Ministry, too, has been controlled for some years by orthodox religious politicians who do not share Kollek's views on the need for sports grounds in various parts of the city.

Despite the recommendations of two independent commissions set up by politicians who backed Kollek's bid for independence, and promises of development funds and separate powers, the Mayor entered the twentieth-anniversary year of the city's reunification without even a grant for the celebrations (later, a modest sum was allotted). The entire City Council walked out in protest, in January 1987, against the government's delays in endorsing payments for debts incurred by the city as the result of the government's building policies and its inflationary financing, back in 1984. By Israeli standards, the city's bookkeeping is exemplary. Jerusalem covers some 70 per cent of its budget from local rates and rarely exceeds its estimated expenditure.

Nevertheless, government officials are reluctant to allow Jerusalem to become an exception in terms of local autonomy. In many capital cities there are tussles for power between the central government and the local authorities, and officials question whether Kollek really wants to be landed with the responsibilities such a transfer would entail. Even so, it is difficult to avoid the impression that there are other reasons why the government has resisted Kollek's demands for so long. As his power and influence have grown internationally, his domestic limitations have come to irk him all the more. During his first years in office, the government often kept him in ignorance of the basic decisions it made on the city. Kollek is not a party politician, though a member of the Labour Party, and he has not, as lesser men have frequently done, used his municipal career as a stepping-stone to national politics. When he was asked by an interviewer in 1985 whether he would consider a cabinet post, he retorted that he doubted whether his Labour colleagues would favour a man who had from the outset opposed the launching of Israel's war in Lebanon. And indeed in his relations with the government it has often appeared that the party politicians were taking their revenge on a man who has made no secret of his disdain for the inter party concerns and has not always kept in line with party policy. While Kollek, for his part, has preferred to maintain his independence as Mayor of Jerusalem, the politicians have continued to rein him in, and civil servants argue that it would not be in the government's interests to increase his statutory power, as the municipal administration itself has no built-in checks and balances.

There is a little park on a hill in the eastern part of the city which overlooks the main road from Ramallah to Jerusalem, with a view towards Mount Scopus. It was here that the fate of the city was decided in June 1967, during a six-hour battle which was one of the most savage in all the Arab–Israel wars, and during which Israeli and Jordanian soldiers struggled in hand-to-hand combat through the twisting trenches of what has since been called Ammunition Hill.

In Jerusalem, where the victors live side by side with the defeated, there is no one great war monument. Instead, scattered along the old frontier and in corners of the eastern city where most of the fighting took place, are memorial plaques for the Israeli dead, decorated each June with fresh wreaths which quickly wither in the summer heat. The Arabs of the city have one war memorial – in the main Moslem cemetery – over which Kollek had one of his first post-war fights in the City Council. While the city was still divided, Israel held military parades in Jerusalem every year, and after the war one more parade was held, which passed through the eastern part of the city against Kollek's wishes.

Now such demonstrations of naked military power have ended; there are only the swearing-in ceremonies of new army recruits at the Western Wall. When the chief of central command during the

Six Day War, Uzi Narkiss, and Yosef Shani, father of one of the soldiers killed in the battle for Jerusalem, came to Kollek for advice on the upkeep of Ammunition Hill, he suggested public tours for American visitors, changes in the layout of the little stage, bands on summer evenings. But he resisted the suggestion for a military museum put forward by someone in the Tel Aviv army headquarters. 'We have enough military symbols in Jerusalem already. We need more music in the parks, something to set against the influence of the [religious] orthodox.'

It is unpleasant for most Israelis to reflect that military power alone has ensured its control of Jerusalem. In 1967 the conquest of the city was seen as the righting of a wrong, the restoration of the Jews to the Old City where for over a century they had been a majority, but where Jews had not ruled since antiquity. Even during the British mandate, the Arab population objected to any but a Moslem mayor. During the 1948 war between Israel and the Arab states, the Jews were driven out of the Old City by the Arab Legion, and Israel was forced to see the city divided with Jordan, but with the Old City's Jewish Quarter excluded. All this was to change when King Hussein decided, against the warning of the Israeli Prime Minister, Levi Eshkol, to join in the war of 1967 between Israel and Egypt. Eshkol had assured the King that Israel would make no first move in Jerusalem, and that the battles raging in the south against Egypt need not spread to the Holy City. Hussein rejected Eshkol's warning and shelled the western city, thus losing both the West Bank and east Jerusalem. Israel, which since 1948 had mourned the loss of its university and hospital on Mount Scopus, the Jewish Quarter and the Western Wall, now saw its chance to regain them.

When the Israelis re-entered the eastern part of the city after nineteen years, they found that the Jordanians had tried systematically to remove all traces of Jewish settlement and history from the city. The ancient Jewish cemetery on the Mount of Olives had been vandalized: a road had been constructed through it and a hotel built on the ridge above it – a site sacred to Christians. Those synagogues in the old Jewish Quarter which had survived the battles of 1948 had been dynamited. When American town planners, together with the Jordanians, framed their proposals for Jerusalem in the 1960s, the Jewish Quarter was scheduled to become a park. Israeli archaeologists, when they revisited the Rockefeller Museum in 1967, where there had been no Jewish visitors since 1948, were amazed to find that all captions to exhibits with the words 'Hebrew' and 'Israelite' had been covered with tape, while road signs with Jewish names had been plastered over.

The Jordanian offensive, and Israel's discovery of the destruction in the Jewish Quarter after the war, played as important a part in subsequent policy making as a sense of history or nationalist fervour. The first thing Israel did in the Old City, apart from restoring basic services, was defiantly to reassert the Jewish presence. The new Israeli law reaffirming the Turkish *status quo* in the Holy Places made one change: it enabled Jews to pray at the Western Wall as of right and not on Moslem sufferance. Those prayers had taken place in a narrow alley between the Moghrabi (Moors) Quarter and the Wall itself. A few days after the end of the war, Kollek ordered the bulldozers in to the Moors Quarter; the residents were hastily evicted and the whole area, a poor district of 106 adobe huts with several hundred inhabitants, was completely razed to create a precinct for Jewish assembly and worship. The whole operation was carried out so rapidly that it took municipal officials weeks to locate the inhabitants, who were camping out in courtyards and abandoned houses, and offer them compensation; it took six months, subsequently, for the government to pay up. In an interview in 1981, Kollek explained that he had ordered the razing of the Moors Quarter entirely on his own responsibility – before the UN, UNESCO or some other hostile international body could intervene.

Later, the Arab tenants of the Jewish Quarter were also moved out, but in a more orderly process. They were rehoused in Arab villages and in a public housing project constructed by Arab contractors with help from the Ministry of Housing. The Jewish Quarter was reconstructed and allotted to Jewish applicants. Only about 5 per cent of those who applied belong to families who had once lived there; but the resettlement was symbolic: the idea was to recreate the former atmosphere of the Quarter in the reconstruction, whose most striking characteristic is its defensive insulation behind high walls. The government declared the Jewish Quarter a national property and carried out its development separately, working through a company in which the municipality had a minority vote.

Meanwhile, the government was taking steps to ensure that Jerusalem would be as difficult as possible to redivide at any future peace conference. The city's boundaries were redrawn with two aims in mind: to hold all the strategic heights around the city, and to ensure, as far as possible, permanent numerical superiority for the Jewish population. Israeli law was introduced in east Jerusalem, and eight Arab villages were included in the newly drawn municipal area. Jerusalem now covered nearly 28,000 acres, more than three times the size of Jewish Jerusalem between 1948 and 1967. The borders sliced through hilltops and encircled defensible valleys, taking much land from Arab villages but excluding many townships in order to keep the official number of Arab residents to just over a quarter of the population at that time. About one-third of the area of the eastern city was expropriated from its Arab owners (no built-up areas were included, however) during the next few years, as Israel began to construct a further fortification, an outer citadel enclosing the historic city within. This was made up of a series of residential suburbs, each as large as a small town, just inside the city's newly enlarged northern, eastern and southern boundaries.

Kollek had joined in the first rush to assert Jewish dominion in the city and to enlarge its municipal boundaries. But his day-to-day experience in running the city, and the reactions from abroad, were soon to make him pause. What Israel had done in Jerusalem had triggered off vigorous international opposition. Israel was accused of changing the nature of the historic city, of wrecking the scale and perspective of old Jerusalem, of foreclosing the options for peace. It was condemned in the Western press, by the Vatican, at UNESCO, and criticized even by the American administration. The opposition reached a climax in 1969 when William Rogers, then Richard Nixon's Secretary of State, suggested that Israel and Jordan should govern the city jointly and that Israel should refrain from making any further unilateral changes.

The result in Jerusalem was that the cement mixers churned even faster. Jerusalem was now to be rebuilt not as a city which develops organically, from the centre outwards, but from the periphery inwards, a process against all urban logic but which followed Israel's long-standing strategy of 'creating facts on the ground'. Urban and aesthetic arguments took second place to rapid development and assertive claims to territory.

Teddy Kollek, as mayor, faced a municipal and political dilemma. He wanted a dense, modernized, compact city centre; and his experience in representing Israel abroad in the past had made him among those most sensitive to the dangers of alienating international public opinion. He and his supporters in the municipality fought a losing battle, between 1967 and 1971, against the construction of huge residential blocks on the periphery which would strain the already over-extended city services to the limit. But eventually he had to fall into line behind the politicians. Rather than appear unpatriotic, he too raised his hand and voted for the new suburbs.

At the same time, he succeeded in deflecting the hail of criticism. While other Israeli politicians traded defiance for reproof, Kollek, in July 1969, founded the Jerusalem Committee. This was a galaxy of leading architects, historians, theologians, philosophers and statesmen from all over the world, whom Kollek roped in as informal advisors on the development of Jerusalem. He invited them all to Jerusalem to see for themselves whether Israel was actually undermining the foundations of the great mosques on the Temple Mount, as the Arab states maintained, or grinding up Moslem architecture to build Jewish housing blocks, as one Mexican architect and town planner said he had been told. They found, of course, nothing of the kind. Government and municipal companies were busy repairing drains and restoring the crumbling foundations of the Old City, and the visitors could see that the remains of Byzantine churches and Moslem buildings were treated no differently from Jewish antiquities. They observed that the Jordanians had built their commercial centre practically up to the Damascus Gate and had permitted the construction of the large Intercontinental Hotel on the Mount of Olives. So in 1969 the seventy wise men of the West issued a statement that they had found Israel 'deeply engaged in rehabilitation work and archaeological exploration' and administered only the mildest of rebukes about 'unco-ordinated planning'.

The plenum of the Committee was not qualified to sit in judgement on Jerusalem planning projects. Kollek was encouraged to go one step further, and summoned a Town Planning sub-committee of architects and planners to the city in December 1970. What he intended this time was to present to them the hastily refurbished Master Plan for the city, originally drafted in its earliest form in the pre-war years, now brought up to date with new highway schemes designed to cope with the huge increase of traffic into Jerusalem since its reunification; it also incorporated several of the features of plans drawn up by British town planners during the mandatory period, who had all recommended a green belt around the Old City and clearly zoned areas for residential and industrial development. Kollek himself knew little about planning, and he clearly hoped to win approval for what Israel was doing.

Kollek's initiative was unprecedented in two respects: he was opening up the planning process of the Israeli capital to foreign critics; and he was also inviting a panel of the world's most famous architects and planners to judge the work of a local team. The results were predictable. The star guests tore the unfortunate local planners to pieces.

Lewis Mumford, Louis Kahn, Bruno Zevi, Denys Lasdun, Buckminster Fuller and many others looked at the plan and saw that it was bad. They told the Mayor, in no uncertain terms, that his plan was a disaster. In looking round the city, they observed the appearance of several high-rise buildings in the western part to which Kollek had been committed by planning committees long before the Six Day War. Where the Master Plan was concerned, they were horrified by the prospect of major roads leading into the city from the west, which would have meant destroying whole neighbourhoods, and a huge clover-leaf exchange situated only yards from the Old City walls. One planner suggested that the Israelis might as well turn Jerusalem into one huge parking lot. Bruno Zevi told Kollek that the city was committing collective hara-kiri. Louis Kahn said that the high-rise buildings appearing in the western town were 'like Indians attacking a wagon train'. The work carried out in the Jewish Quarter was termed 'kitsch' and the new suburbs under construction out of scale with the rest of the city. They could see no 'unified theme', no sensible provision for intercity transportation; they criticized many features of the plan which were dictated by the existence of not one but two Jerusalems, which had been self-contained only three and a half years earlier. They called for more public participation in the planning process, at a time when Jerusalem's environmentalists were only just getting into their stride. They recommended that the city commission a three-dimensional model so that the planners could see what they were doing, and that Kollek set up an effective city planning office with a qualified planner in charge. (The Master Plan office, set up before the unification of the city, was financed by the government and those involved were the Ministry of Housing, the Lands Authority and the Ministry of Transport.)

Kollek managed to ensure that the statement eventually published was a watered-down version of the stormy committee meeting. Fortunately the Hebrew press ignored the visitors almost completely. After a world-wide search for the experienced planner whose presence was regarded as essential in the city by the Jerusalem Committee, the city found a distinguished expert in the economics of planning, Professor Nathaniel Lichfield, who was appointed Chief City Planner working with the City Engineer's office in May 1972, and took up his appointment for an eighteen-month initial term in June of that year. He formulated a new overall planning concept for the city which was warmly received at the Jerusalem Committee's Town Planning sub-committee in May 1973. Fuller, 'dismayed' in 1970, was by 1973 convinced that the newly established Urban Planning Unit was 'going for the right things'. Kahn and Lasdun were brought in to submit designs for the Hurva synagogue in the Jewish Quarter – though neither was finally accepted. Bruno Zevi defended the restorers of Jerusalem against the *Osservatore Romano*, reminding Italian Catholics that the Byzantine remains at the heart of the Jewish Quarter had been preserved, while Jewish antiquities in the Vatican were neglected.

In fact, by 1972 the second huge suburb within the extended borders, French Hill (now renamed Givat Shapira), had covered one hill in sight of the Old City. At the same time the Hebrew University was wrecking the summit of Mount Scopus with a new campus planned, by a committee of some of Israel's most distinguished architects, as a fortress approached from the west by turnstiles, gloomy, echoing bus tunnels and ground level car parks. But there were signs of hope. Some of the more megalomaniac plans for central Jerusalem for tunnels, bridges and towers had been shelved; the Master Plan was revamped and the over-ambitious road scheme modified. When, in 1974, UNESCO blasted Israel's reconstruction in the Old City, the Jerusalem Committee urged it to continue 'in the interests of mankind'.

Ultimately, however, it was not the critics on the Jerusalem Committee who saved the central area of Jerusalem, but the 1973 war. This, and the ensuing period of economic austerity, restored planning for Jerusalem to more natural and modest proportions — save, of course, for the continuing construction of the outer citadel of densely designed suburbs. The 1973 war had reinforced Israel's fear of attack from without and once more jogged the building reflexes of the Ministry of Housing. But this was beyond Kollek's control.

The Mayor was left with the problem of the restoration and beautification plans for the neglected centre of the city, and the desire to improve Jerusalem's cultural facilities. The forestry commission, the Keren Kayemet, was planting a green belt round Jerusalem, but the government was spending all its resources on the outer suburbs. So Kollek bypassed both the government and his municipal limitations by means of the Jerusalem Foundation, a private corporation which had begun, quite modestly, on the eve of his first election in 1965, as a campaign chest financed by his friends abroad.

Even before he thought of becoming mayor, Kollek had acquired great experience in both public and private fund-raising for cultural purposes. He had established the Israel Museum, inaugurated in 1965, during a period when immigrants were still being housed in huts and asbestos shacks. The nucleus of this museum had existed for years, in the shape of a small collection of Judaica and oriental exhibits assembled by Mordechai Narkiss, founder of the old Bezalel museum in the centre of town, and archaeological finds from Israeli excavations in the care of the government Department of Antiquities. To this had been added, over the years, a number of paintings by local artists and works of art brought to Israel by refugees from Europe. Kollek decided that Jerusalem needed a museum of world class, and resented the fact that wealthy Jews abroad never thought of donating even a part of their collections to Israel.

Today the museum, with its ever-expanding pavilions, houses not only local antiquities, Judaica and Israeli art, but a reconstructed Italian synagogue, a Louis XVI salon contributed by the French Rothschilds, collections of ethnography, pre-Columbian art, Impressionists and a collection of Old Masters, a sculpture garden and a youth wing. This has special exhibitions for children and classes in everything from ceramics to mime, and is visited by schoolchildren from every part of the city; east Jerusalem children also have an annexe at the Rockefeller Museum just outside the Old City. Kollek has remained, throughout his time as mayor, chairman of the board of directors of the Israel Museum. His address books are a directory of the world's great philanthropists.

Kollek was also involved, during the early years of the state, in establishing Israel Bonds, and he knew all the legal and bureaucratic problems involved in raising money from philanthropists funding state organizations. Under American law, no tax exemption could be granted to those who gave money directly to a public organization; and on the Israeli side, money given by individuals to funds like the United Jewish Appeal disappeared into the Israeli Treasury. Donors were unable to pinpoint the exact results of their donations. The Jerusalem Foundation was a new departure.

Individual donors were found for specific projects within the city. Kollek's priorities were parks, cultural centres and synagogues (initially in the Old City), and the restoration projects going on in the Old City, on the one hand; and community centres, sports grounds and welfare projects in the working-class areas of the city, on the other. The Jerusalem Foundation gave the donors the feeling that they were participating directly in the building of the city, and served a shrewd political purpose within Jerusalem itself – even though its local beneficiaries were not always able to distinguish clearly between the Foundation and other private charities. The Foundation grew fast – from a small office in the municipal buildings to an independent organization with voluntary committees in half a dozen countries, and in Israel its own technical staff and contractors. Speed was essential. Donors wanted to see quick results, the Foundation to capitalize on pledges before the donors changed their minds, or died (many were retired millionaires). All over the city, the sign of the Foundation appeared: small pillars and larger dice blocks, inscribed with the Foundation's logo – a crenellated tulip.

All through the autumn of 1986, a promenade of expensively chiselled Jerusalem stone, punctuated by stone alcoves with wooden pergolas, and supported by a series of structures resembling a Roman aqueduct, was constructed along the ridge to the south-west of the city, the former demilitarized zone between the centre and the Hill of Evil Counsel. Nearby, yet another park was inaugurated for the new suburb of East Talpiot, with at its centre a mosaic floor illustrating the underground aqueduct which linked Jerusalem and the country-side to the southern hills at the time of the Second Temple. Kindergar-tens, tennis-courts and community centres were opened in the new suburbs. And work proceeded on yet another museum, this time one over which Kollek had fought a long battle with many of his subordi-nates in the municipality: the city museum at the Citadel.

The Citadel, like other national sites formerly in the possession of the Jordanian government, is the property of the Israel Lands Auth-ority. Its excavation was soon undertaken by the city's archaeologists, who uncovered the Hasmonean foundations deep below the Herodian ruins as well as inspected the successive Roman, Byzantine, Mame-luke, Crusader and Ottoman additions. The site was very soon the delight of archaeologists but the despair of everyone else, from the City Council to UNESCO, to whom it seemed less a historic site than an inexplicable obstacle course. The Lands Authority, at Kollek's prompting, leased it to the Jerusalem Foundation, which had found an English benefactor who was prepared to back its renovation. Every-one was agreed that the Citadel was important as the main entry point to the historic city, near the Jaffa Gate, and ideally suited as a city museum. But here the disagreements started.

Senior officials in the municipality wanted the Citadel Museum to be run by the city. But Kollek was determined to recruit designers of world class, and chose his own team, headed by an English expert, Professor Gardner, who had planned the very successful Diaspora Museum in Tel Aviv, as well as other famous displays abroad. At the Israel Museum, Kollek had always allowed his curators to decide policy, and in the case of the Citadel, he consulted a team of academic advisors to vet the first blueprints. Several, however, found the multi-media approach altogether too popular for their taste — as one put it, a 'Disneyland' version of the city's history — and withdrew in protest. But with his millionaire donor behind him, Kollek went ahead.

Pending its transformation, the Citadel is at present a backdrop for sound and light displays. Visitors enter by the main gate, descend deep into grassy moats, ascend dizzying towers, wander across battlements and along parapets labelled tersely with dates and names, and study a scale model of nineteenth-century Jerusalem recently discovered in Geneva. In October 1986, Kollek reviewed progress on the proposed museum: a multi-route exhibition leading across the site past three-dimensional models and perspex cases in which the history of the city is reviewed, from Canaanite times to the State of Israel in 'sequential visualization'.

Kollek and advisors, with the help of slides, ponder the problematic balance of research and graphic display. The Mayor wants to be reassured that the three-dimensional model of the Jebusite city is based on up-to-date archaeological research, and that rabbis are consulted on whether the 'Diorama of the Ark brought to Jerusalem' may not offend the orthodox. A model of the First Temple is to be flanked by video systems, conveying the experience of the High Priest entering the precincts. Kollek wants to know what the scholars think about this, what evidence there is behind the display. Karl Katz of the New York Metropolitan Museum, in his youth director of the Bezalel museum, suggests that a leaflet can be distributed at the entrance, with the latest information on dissenting scholarly opinion.

The 'visual gaps' in Jerusalem's ancient history gape as wide as the moats and ditches in the Citadel. The designers have bridged them with blow-ups of well-known Renaissance paintings. 'Four-fifths of the elements in Western thought are based on biblical history,' the literary advisor has calculated. 'Good,' says Kollek. 'The universality of Jerusalem, that's what we want, something that justifies pluralism today.'

Dioramas display the Maccabeans purifying the Temple in Hellenistic times and the Roman siege of the Herodian city. Officials of the city and the Foundation are relieved to recognize ruins recently restored in the Old City: the Cardo, the Roman arcade now a line of exclusive boutiques, and the Nea Church, one apse of which now lies in an illuminated cellar close by the rebuilt rabbinical seminaries of the Jewish Quarter. Exhibits illustrating the spread of Islam and Mohammed's night journey from Jerusalem lead Kollek to observe that little during all those centuries refers to the Jews. 'How do you show the continuity of the Jewish presence during this long period?' he asks. No one has an answer.

But it is during the review of the Crusader period that Kollek really shows his displeasure. An illuminated painting indicates that the Moslem Dome of the Rock, in Crusader times a church named 'Templum Domini', is suddenly topped by a cross. Is this authentic? The Mayor is assured that it is. But here he draws the line. There will be Arab visitors to the exhibition, he protests, and there is no way that they will accept crosses on their great Moslem shrine. The Crusaders' cross will have to go.

Jerusalem rebuilt, modernized, fortified, a new citadel, is not quite impregnable. Over twenty years, Kollek has repeatedly emphasized that the city is a safer place, whether for its residents or for tourists, than any big city in the West. In terms of crime, this is true; political violence is less predictable.

In October 1986, a group of newly recruited soldiers appeared at the Western Wall for one of the swearing-in ceremonies which are regularly held there. 'Only those who know how to defend their freedom deserve it' was the legend on the invitation distributed to parents who had lined up to watch their sons take the oath, and then accompanied them to the buses waiting to take them back to army bases. The parking lot is just outside the nearby Dung Gate, and beyond it, the Arab village of Silwan.

From this village came three young men, members of a self-styled Islamic Liberation cell, with ties to the PLO. Through contacts encountered on a visit to a mosque in Amman, it had taken them a year and a half to plan the attack on the soldiers at the Dung Gate. From behind a low wall separating the parking lot from the village, they lobbed a clutch of grenades towards the buses. Sixty-nine people, soldiers and civilians, including children, were wounded. One man – the father of one of the soldiers – was killed.

The aftermath of the incident followed what has now become a pattern. Tens of Arab youths were arrested, and in all the Arab villages nearby there were house-to-house searches. The next morning, municipal workers swept up the broken glass and hosed down the bloodstains. Kollek visited the wounded in the city's hospitals. An attack on a military target is rare enough; the army and police exchanged recriminations about faulty security. By mid morning next day there was little trace of the incident save for the shuttered kiosks at the

normally busy corner where Silwan faces the Dung Gate, and some
fragments of broken glass which caught the sun at the road's edge.
Crowds of Israelis swarmed through the Gate on their way to the
Wall, including bar mitzvah boys carried on their fathers' shoulders.
A guide explained to a slightly apprehensive group of tourists, 'It
happens sometimes. We don't pay too much attention. It's a way
of life.'

But in fact one incident like this sets back the tourist trade by
several weeks. Kollek, explaining the harm it did to their livelihood,
called on the heads of the Arab communities in the city to denounce
terror, but they did not. Acts like the attack at the Dung Gate are
seen by most Arabs in the city as resistance, not as terror.

Kollek, an old-fashioned liberal of the European school, has always
traced violent crime – even political crime – to poverty and ignorance.
He continually argues that the government's failure to provide money
for more school buildings and housing for the city's Arabs is raising
a generation of terrorists. The Hebrew press took much the same
line the day after the attack in articles about Silwan; conditions in
the village, ran the headlines, make young men turn to violence. On
the other hand, every paper quoted the fact that the mother of the
notorious terrorist Abu Musa lives in Silwan and is paid Israeli national insurance.

Silwan is a famous village, built on the margin of the Valley of
Kidron. It is a tourist site with its underground stream and fountain,
'Siloa's Brook', the biblical Shiloah, and the Graeco Roman tomb
popularly known as that of Absalom. Silwan's fame is a mixed blessing for its residents. It brings a few score tourists to buy soft drinks
and postcards, but its central place in the ancient necropolis surrounding the Old City has proved unfortunate. In 1974, the Rabbinate
discovered that ancient Jewish graves lay beneath the main access
road through the valley, and insisted that it be closed to traffic. The
city financed an alternative road. The villagers also did not welcome
the attention of archaeologists who had found that the eastern slope
was pitted with ancient burial caves, many of which are used by
the villagers as barns or stables.

Silwan is not only a country village. It is also an urban slum, whose
worst problem is overcrowding. Descendants of the original families
are outnumbered by refugees from the 1948 war, evacuees from the

Jewish Quarter in 1967, and migrant workers from Hebron and elsewhere in the West Bank. Some of the Silwan people have left for the Gulf States, from which they send money back to their families. Most of those who remain work in the day on building sites, in hotels and in workshops in the city, returning to the village at night. Silwan has produced several distinguished families, but also more than its share of pickpockets, drug pedlars and boys who cannot find any regular work. They are always the first suspects in roundups by the police and the security forces after a terrorist attack, as were the young men of the Islamic Liberation cell.

In this case the three offenders were caught within twenty-four hours. Two of them had often traded information to the police about drug pedlars and thieves. They were so confident of their alibis that they drove to the police headquarters in the Russian Compound on the day after the attack, promising fresh leads on drug traffic. What they did not know was that the number of their Volvo – bought with PLO funds – which they had used the previous night, had been spotted next to the Dung Gate.

Kollek and the Foundation have had plans to improve conditions in Silwan for years. There is no legal outline plan as yet for the villages, and permits for new houses are rarely granted, though some live packed ten to a room in outhouses, shacks and even caves. There is no slum clearance project for Arabs in Jerusalem. Silwan is not a government priority, and rehousing is problematic here. As in most Arab districts, each plot of land has been parcelled and reparcelled between families over generations, and Arabs are deeply suspicious of any Israeli attempts to requisition any part of an individual holding in order to plan a housing project.

The city financed an Israeli architect to design a scheme by which new houses would be threaded in to the gaps between existing buildings; the Foundation is prepared to help financially. But the plan, with many others relating to the Arab population, has been held up for months by the District Planning Committee. If a start is not made soon, says the architect, the plan, negotiated with so much difficulty between various families, will be rejected and the villagers will start building on their own again, without permits, risking the destruction of their work if they are spotted by a municipal inspector.

A few days after the capture of the terrorists, the final ritual punishment took place – the sealing, with concrete blocks in windows and bars welded across the doors, of the houses where the terrorists' families live. This form of collective punishment, first introduced by the British authorities during the mandate, is milder than that imposed in the West Bank, officially occupied territory and not under Israeli law. There, houses are dynamited. After 1967 this was the procedure in Jerusalem as well, but Kollek protested and achieved a compromise by which the houses were only sealed. Now, for Silwan, choking on its own inhabitants, Kollek made a special plea and gained a further concession: only the rooms actually occupied by the offenders were closed off from the rest of the building.

A few weeks after the attack on the Dung Gate, undeterred by fire or flood, like troops to the relief of a besieged city, came one of the largest single tourist groups to visit Jerusalem in recent years: supporters of the International Christian Embassy.

Its origins were curious. After 1977, with Menachem Begin's right wing in power, the government defied world opinion and once more asserted Israel's exclusive claims to Jerusalem. In 1980, the newly militant far-right parties tabled a law reasserting Israel's position on the city, the 'Jerusalem Law'. The immediate protests from abroad rallied even those Israeli Knesset members who had initially opposed the law as provocative and gratuitous. It was passed by an overwhelming majority: 99 to 15. Kollek, who thought the law unnecessary, a typically empty gesture by a government which did little in practice to improve the city's status, made his own contribution to its formulation through his colleagues in the Labour Party. Two extra clauses were added: one, much watered down by Begin, reaffirming the fact that access to the Holy Places of all faiths was guaranteed by Israel; the other, that the government was henceforth committed to increased financial support of the city. There was no dramatic increase of government funds to the municipal budget, however, and the first of Kollek's clauses had no effect on international opinion.

The majority of those countries which recognized the State of Israel (though not Jerusalem as its capital, or Israeli rule of east Jerusalem) had always maintained embassies in Tel Aviv. These included the United States, Britain and most European countries. However, there were several countries which, until the passage of the Jerusalem Law, had none the less established embassies in the Jewish capital. These included the Netherlands — the only European country to do so — and Turkey, the only Moslem state in the region without an ideological commitment against Israel. No sooner was the law passed than thirteen embassies (including these two) packed up and left for Tel Aviv.

Shortly after the thirteen embassies made their grand exit, a group of Protestant Evangelical Christians opened the 'International Christian Embassy' in a walk-up flat in a Jerusalem suburb. Before long these 'Christian Zionists' had convened 'A Christian Celebration during the Feast of Tabernacles in the City of the Great King'. Bemused Israelis now became accustomed to the sight of cohorts of Scandinavian, Philippine, South American and other pilgrims marching through the streets of central Jerusalem dressed in national costume, waving flags and proclaiming their solidarity with Jewish Jerusalem.

In 1985 they sponsored an International Christian Zionist Congress at Basle, site of Herzl's first great rally in 1897. In Jerusalem, every autumn, they take over the National Convention Centre. Binyanei HaOomah, at the entrance to Jerusalem, next door to the Hilton Hotel, and hold sessions of 'Davidic Worship', faith healing sessions, and a Praise Procession from the Mount of Olives to the Old City. This is different from the conventional Palm Sunday procession in that the marchers do not only commemorate Christ's entry into Jerusalem. They look forward to the imminent return of the King of Kings and Messiah of Israel, which they believe has been signalled by recent history.

So at Tabernacles, fifteen hundred Christian Zionists pack the conference hall at their festive opening. On the platform, an enormous red and gold crown dangles over the bandstand, and a giant seven-branched candlestick indicates the participants' pro-Jewish sentiments. Banners hung round the balconies read 'The Lord Chose Jerusalem', 'We Come to Speak Comfort to Zion' and 'Behold I will bring them from the North Country' — a reference to Soviet Jewry, for whom the Christian Zionists also campaign. Supplies of grain, it is said, have been stockpiled by their workers in ancient castles across Europe against what they see as the coming Exodus of Jews from Russia.

Within seconds of the country-music band tuning up, the audience has already reached a high pitch of enthusiasm. The programme discourages public utterances from the floor: 'If you believe you have a word from God, please submit it to Speakers' Panel.' After a mere two verses of 'Come to the Mountain of the Lord' half the Davidic worshippers are already on their feet, eyes closed and hands raised in affirmation, keeping up a gentle, windscreen-wiper motion. Lights flicker on them from the stage, and a tiny tinkling comes from the little brass bells some of the worshippers have tied to their fingers.

The first speaker of the evening is the Mayor, who is given a huge ovation as 'a friend of Christians for many years', and he responds to it like an old trouper, with what is for Kollek an amazingly long speech: eight minutes.

'Thanks for the welcome; we'd like it at election time.' [Appreciative laughter.] After a few introductory words of greeting, he was off on his usual pitch: 'Like your first song says, you have come to the Mountain of the Lord ... many of you come from homogeneous cities and countries ... this is a pluralist city ... in Jerusalem there are forty different Christian denominations ... the Catholics, Johnnies-come-lately ... it wasn't always a free and open city ... on our side, no one could visit the Holy Places. Ninety per cent of the city is religious. ... Every year we have five to six hundred thousand Christian visitors. Terror made it more difficult. ... You all deserve a medal! [The audience agrees with him, riotous applause.] More people are killed in car accidents in a day in New York than in a year here [more applause].'

The Mayor now turns to archaeology, in which he takes a particular interest. 'In this city archaeologists have to research a site before we can build. In one house we found Turkish rifles from the First World War – a little deeper we found the floor of a Byzantine church – then Jewish graves from the First Temple Period. They'd all been robbed, but in one we found two silver scrolls. It took us a year to unroll them. We found – the same blessing we use today! [Gasps from the audience.] We'd been away two thousand years and came back according to prophecy [vigorous applause]. We are the only people in this area who speak Isaiah's language! [Frenetic applause.] Our friends have to bear with our mistakes ... statebuilding is a difficult business. There are in Jerusalem one hundred and two Jewish groups, forty Christian sects ... Arabs from all over ... to bring this together is a task for more than one generation and friends are necessary. Write postcards and tell people what they missed! [Wild applause.] The Christian Embassy gives us all strength and courage ... I thank you very much.' (Kollek exits left.)

With the departure of the Mayor, the Davidic worshippers proceed with the serious business of the evening, the Seminar on Healing. This is given by a Florida preacher of Indian parentage, Mahesh Chavda, who explained the wonder of the 'strategic era' for Israel and the Church militant, in which the fortunes of Israel are to be restored and the Remnant to return. At enormous length, he tells of miracles in Finland and witchcraft in Zaire, which failed when confronted with the power of God in Chavda's own person; of prayer sessions in the caucus room of the House of Representatives in Washington; and of Europe preparing for the Exodus of the Jews from Russia, the place of the Throne of Satan, where 'Chernobyl was just the beginning of the Plagues!' 'They couldn't drink the water a thousand kilometres from Kiev!' Chavda tells his spellbound audience. 'The plague is visited on the persecutors of Israel. God will deliver his people!'

There are cries of 'Right on! Halleluja! Praise the Lord!' The lights on the stage winked on and off, amplifiers magnify the Lord, and the little bells tinkle the assent of the multitude.

Israeli leaders, from the Prime Minister to the politically minded rabbis, publicly welcome the Christian Zionists' arrival, either unaware of, or deciding to ignore the fact that the return of the Christian Messiah is invariably linked, in Evangelical eschatology, with the conversion of the Jews. The Christian Zionists' declared policy is to support all the conquests of 1967 as belonging to Israel by right, for reasons of biblical precedent. They warn Israel against any compromise on the West Bank and even urge it to claim its rights on the Temple Mount. Kollek, well to the left of Israel's political spectrum, has nevertheless decided to ignore this as something, he says, 'of concern to American liberals'. 'We can't reject friends,' he adds. Jim Bakker, the television preacher, (before he was defrocked and disgraced) pledged an Evangelical group to raise funds for a park in east Jerusalem. Kollek is not about to turn away admirers who proclaim that they 'like the way God works through him'.

2

The View from the Mayor's Office

THE JERUSALEM CITY COUNCIL chamber is a very grand room for such a shabby building, with mottled black marble pillars, stained-glass windows, wood panelling and a dais at one end. It was formerly the main hall of Barclays Bank, and presents its shell-pocked façade to the north-west corner of the Old City walls, a few yards away from City Hall. Here Kollek receives the city's Christian hierarchy (not at Christmas, but at Chanuka, the Jewish festival of lights, anniversary of the Maccabean victory). Here, he receives the largest foreign delegations: in autumn 1986 there were the burghers of Dinkelsbühl in Bavaria, and the Mexican Knights of Columbus. On such occasions he is received with spontaneous applause.

No applause greets Kollek when he strides into the monthly meeting of the City Council. His place is not on the dais where the stenographers sit but at one end of the huge oval table, where he sits impatiently sucking on his cigar and waving his gavel, prodding, the Council through its long agenda with his eye on his watch.

As Mayor, Teddy Kollek has had no rivals. Municipal elections in Israel are held every five years and generally on a party political basis. Until 1978, votes were cast only for a party (or local factional) list. At that date, however, direct elections for the mayor himself were introduced, separately from the vote for his party – a veritable revolution in Israel's political scene, where there are no constituency elections and the proportional representation system is dominated by powerful central party committees.

Even before 1978, Kollek's personality won him the leading role in the city – first as head of a small breakaway faction from Labour (Rafi, Ben Gurion's splinter party) and then as head of the Labour list. Nevertheless, when proposals are put to the vote, he is faced with a City Council which reflects in its composition the strength of the right wing and religious parties in the city. Since direct elections were introduced on a personal basis, Kollek has won two-thirds of the votes for mayor. But as head of the Council, he has a bare majority. It is thus that he explains to visitors: 'It's easier for a Republican President to govern Congress and Senate with a Democratic majority than it is for me to run the City Council without an absolute majority.'

But the real irony of the situation is that Kollek owes that bare majority, in the present coalition, to the small but significant Arab vote. The city's Arabs, as foreign citizens, are not entitled to vote at national elections, but as permanent residents of the city, by a special ruling introduced not long after the 1967 war, they are qualified to vote at municipal elections. Although only some 20 per cent of those entitled to do so use this right, it is the roughly two and a half seats on the Council they contribute to One Jerusalem, Kollek's faction since 1978, which allows him to dominate city policy.

Where the day-to-day running of the municipal departments is concerned, Kollek has managed to appoint men and women to run the city on the basis of professional skills alone. He has chased party politics out of the offices, but he cannot outlaw politics from the Council chamber. Here, One Jerusalem faces the constant opposition of the right-wing Likud group (Herut, Begin's old party, and the Liberals) and the ultra-orthodox Agudat Israel, conspicuous in their heavy beards and black silk frock-coats. Here, issues are not discussed on their merits but according to a predetermined political stand. Every pension paid to a municipal employee, every road dug up more than once to lay pipes, even the problem of where to put the city's dead (west Jerusalem has run out of cemetery space) becomes an excuse for a political line-up and often for a formal vote. At any given moment, the Likud will goad the Mayor like picadors in the ring. But there is no matador.

Everyone knows Kollek is unbeatable. Before the last elections, the Herut leadership decided that, unable to defeat Kollek, they would try, on every occasion, to limit his power. The Agudat Israel, for many years Kollek's coalition partners, now in opposition, are there primarily to ask for more for their 'holy public': more synagogue space, more ritual baths, more grants for seminaries; and to protest at every attempt to infringe the Sabbath in the city: cinema shows, restaurants or cafés open. Kollek's own faction, made up mainly of Labour supporters in the city but with a number of public figures, responds laconically to the rhetoric of the Likud and the Agudat Israel. They leave it to Kollek to provide the drama: at what point, precisely, will the Mayor lose his famous temper?

The only point on which the Council is always of one mind is

anger at the unwillingness of the government to help the city financially. The city carries out national functions which demand expenditure over and above that of normal city administration. The first
item on the agenda is a demand that the Housing Ministry finance
maintenance of public institutions at Pisgat Ze'ev, the last of the
huge peripheral suburbs now under construction.

Then the picadors advance, the first prick of the lance is delivered:
the Fast Hotel. Nearly twenty years ago, Kollek's municipality bought
this old property from the Armenian church. Kollek encouraged an
American investor to plan a three-storey hotel on the site, a triangle
of land opposite the Old City walls. Years passed, planning concepts
changed, the site changed hands and Kollek changed his mind. But
he had promised the development rights to a second investor, who
dug his heels in. No one really wants or needs the hotel any more,
but to compensate the investor would cost millions in municipal
funds. The Herut councillors rub this in. Kollek fumes and bangs
his gavel as soon as the speaker's statutory four minutes are ended.

The first picador repelled, another comes forward: Jerusalem has
no industrial economy, people are leaving the city for lack of jobs,
the Mayor is at fault. Kollek tightens his lips round his cigar: the
taunt is answered by one of the city's leading factory owners, with
facts and figures. Everyone knows that Kollek has done what he
can to bring high-tech industry to the capital, and factory space has
more than doubled over the last few years.

Now it is the turn of the Agudat Israel leader, Rabbi Meir Porush,
son of one of Kollek's former allies, head of the Agudat Israel party
in the Knesset, Rabbi Menachem Porush. Porush Senior and Kollek
have recently fallen out, and are involved in an acrimonious corres-
pondence in which Porush continually reminds Kollek of his age (both
men are in their seventies) and Kollek threatens continually to answer
no more letters, though goaded by their content into having the last
word. What Kollek particularly resents is that though the ultra-orthodox political strength in the Knesset gets them government funds,
and though he has been more than generous towards them, they
are never satisfied. Kollek, in his turn, is sharply criticized by the
secular Jewish community for his indulgence towards the orthodox.

Porush Junior, in a plaintive voice, now describes the sad plight
of three hundred orthodox maidens studying in improvised class-

rooms because Kollek will not requisition land for a school. The orthodox schools are private institutions, outside the municipal framework. Kollek removes his cigar and pauses: 'I shall do all I can to help that very quiet and well-behaved community,' he says mildly. The hint is obvious. There has been ultra-orthodox violence and vandalism this autumn in the city.

A Herut councillor reads a telegram from the association of builders and contractors. They are disturbed to learn that a foreign company is going to construct the new municipal complex shortly to rise nearby. Kollek's factory-owner colleague, head of the public committee for the new municipality and City Square, explains that there will be plenty of work for everyone. Kollek hoped to receive a gift to bridge the difference between the value of the property the city hall occupies and the cost of the new complex. The project is necessary, as many municipal offices (including finance and education) are at present scattered throughout the city.

Meanwhile chief picador, matador presumptive – Reuven Rivlin, Herut lawyer, head of the local branch – has sharpened his lance. He presses the request for a square in the centre of town to be named after five Jewish fighters who fell in 1948 at Deir Yassin. An Arab village where more than two hundred men, women and children were killed by the right-wing Jewish militias, Deir Yassin, provoked the flight of thousands of Arabs from Jewish Palestine and has been a key issue in Arab propaganda ever since.

Kollek's answer is measured at first. For the good of the state, he says, Deir Yassin should be forgotten. The current tranquillity in the city is illusory and could be shattered at any moment. 'Why help our enemies?'

Rivlin accuses Kollek of being 'ashamed' of Deir Yassin, 'apologetic' towards the outside world. The implication is that Kollek is less than a patriot. Kollek's voice rises: 'All Israelis are blamed for Deir Yassin, and for Sabra and Shatilla. Jerusalem is in a more delicate position than any other city in Israel.' There is uproar from the Likud and Agudat Israel councillors. The city reporters dozing on their bench lean forward.

Kollek bangs furiously with his gavel and thunders: 'I can judge this better than you. My judgement is better than yours, better than anyone's in this room. I know better than you!' Protesting, but out-shouted, the right wing subsides. Kollek, they know, has a majority on the city's 'names committee', which decides the naming and renaming of districts, streets and squares. The incident is closed.

Three questions can be asked about Teddy Kollek as he presides over the Jerusalem City Council. One: how is it that Jerusalem, which at national elections is a right-wing stronghold, continues to vote for Kollek, associated all his life with the Israeli left wing? Two: how does a man who is not an observant Jew control a city with a constantly increasing ultra-orthodox minority? Three: how does a Zionist politician like Kollek come to owe his slender majority in the City Council to the thousands of votes provided by the Arabs of the city?

The short answer is that while factional politics could rip the city apart, only a strong man who appears to stand above party politics can govern. But this is only part of the explanation.

The head of the Likud faction, Rivlin, has said that there is nothing Kollek has done in Jerusalem that the Likud could not put its name to. But Kollek has made concessions to the reality of a city shared with the Arabs which the Likud, prisoners of their own rhetoric, silently assented to but could not have proposed themselves. No less a supporter of free enterprise than his Likud competitors, and as critical of the welfare state, Kollek has managed to outflank the Likud's populist appeal by appearing as chief benefactor to the city, bringing both bread and circuses.

For the ultra-orthodox Jews, Kollek is the *gvir*, the strong man of the Jewish community who represents them in the Gentile world – a task which they have neither the desire nor the ability to fulfil. He has been no less generous to the orthodox than any of his colleagues in the Labour camp, and not only for political reasons. He declares that their children have the same claim on municipal help for schooling as anyone else. The present coldness between Kollek and the rabbis comes from the fact that the escalation of orthodox demands threatens the character of Kollek's Jerusalem as a cultural metropolis, and not from a lack of willingness, on his part, to allow them a share of his 'multi-ethnic', pluralist city.

Kollek's policy towards the Arabs of Jerusalem has allowed them to maintain their non-recognition of Israeli sovereignty, while at the same time exploiting all the social, economic and legal resources of Israel. The Arab vote at municipal elections, which represents some 20 per cent of those eligible, is only one sign of the tacit understanding that open resistance would penalize, in the first instance, the Arabs themselves. It is no small part of that understanding that Kollek knows how much and how little the votes really mean. They are an acknowledgement that, under a different mayor, the present compromise might be impossible to maintain.

But it is only possible to make all these assessments in retrospect. Looking back, it appears that Kollek's success in Jerusalem has depended on his having been in office at a specific moment in history, a moment which he was uniquely equipped to exploit.

It is a commonplace to argue that Jerusalem before 1967 was stagnant, provincial and undynamic; but this is only partially true. West, Jewish Jerusalem doubled its population between 1948 and 1967, from about 100,000 to nearly 200,000. Arab Jerusalem's population remained stable at around 70,000. In 1948 the city was divided along the ceasefire lines, and west Jerusalem expanded out into the western hills. The old university campus at Scopus was an enclave in Jordanian territory, visited once a fortnight by an Israeli detachment travelling in armoured cars. Jewish philanthropists abroad donated the money to build an alternative campus in the western city. Determined to assert the claim even to half of Jerusalem as its capital, Israel built a government centre and a new parliament building, near the new university. It is for this reason that the visitor will find no great squares or national monuments at the centre of the city: the Old City is an historic, but not a functional, centre.

Arab Jerusalem, having nowhere to go but the desert to the south and east, ribboned out along the hilltops towards Ramallah. Though the home of many leading Palestinian families, it was an ancestral retreat rather than a dynamic centre. It survived essentially as a tourist city, living off the mosques and churches at its heart. Both sides regretted the loss of their homes across a hostile frontier, but there were changes in the population, in both east and west. While many of the more enterprising younger Palestinians left to work and study elsewhere in the Arab world, most of the Jewish increase in the city was due to the successive waves of immigration – from Arab countries and, to a minor degree, from Eastern Europe, during the 1950s and early 1960s.

Before 1967, Jewish Jerusalem had two distinct population groups. There were the veteran, established, predominantly middle-class Jerusalemites, mostly of Western origin but with a few élite Sephardi families. And there were the new immigrants, most of whom represented not the leadership and professional middle classes from the towns of Arab countries, but the artisan and small shopkeeper class who in Israel became the new proletariat. Housed in drab housing estates on the western outskirts, or along the dangerous frontier, or in houses abandoned by Arab refugees in 1948, they slowly rebuilt their lives during a period of economic austerity, helped only by state welfare and a fiercely egalitarian educational system. This system gradually enforced the social integration of all schoolchildren save those of the ultra-orthodox community. This minority huddled together in the older neighbourhoods established at the end of the last century and in a few new housing projects near them. They kept within closely defined areas save when they sallied out – as they did just before Kollek's election in 1965 – to block main roads and stop traffic on the Jewish Sabbath.

Jewish Jerusalem was a poor city whose annual budget barely covered basic services. It was the only large town in Israel which, when its City Council fell apart in the 1950s, was run by a government appointed committee. It was cut off from the rest of the country, accessible only via a long, winding corridor through the hills, and lacked all appeal to tourists. Its only Christian attraction was the village of Ein Karem, birthplace of John the Baptist. The appeal of this village however was soon diversified when it was partnered by the nearby Hadassah medical complex, built to replace the abandoned hospital on Scopus.

The notorious frontier was an attraction of a perverse kind, though not one advertised on the hotel billboards, which suggested Yemenite folk-dancing and Bible quizzes. There were the roads ending in anti-sniper walls, warning signs rusting at the edges of minefields, sand-bagged positions on the corners of the Old City walls, the occasional burst of small-arms fire to interrupt the dark, silent nights, and the clandestine look-out points: the roof of the Notre Dame hospice, from which voyeurs of the eastern city could peer out through a line of washing over fields into Salah ed-Din Street, and the roof of the City Hall, where Kollek would take visitors to look over into the Old City.

This was the city which Teddy Kollek inherited in 1965. And until the 1967 war, as a close aide put it, 'he was the most bored man in the world'.

Although Teddy Kollek grew up in Vienna in the world of the left-wing Zionist youth movements, and spent his earliest years in Israel as treasurer of a newly founded kibbutz on the Sea of Galilee, he is a maverick figure in Israeli politics. Nothing he has said or done bears the mark of a specific ideology. He defines himself as a Zionist with Jewish values and a solid bourgeois background. During the 1930s and 1940s, he played no discernible part in the endless theoretical debates about political 'streams' in state education, or the trade union economy versus private enterprise. But in one respect he is a true son of Labour Zionism. Kollek is, in untranslatable Hebrew slang, a *bitzuist*, a doer, a filler of vacuums, a man always in search of a hole to dig or a stockade to put up, or – in his youth – a sack of gravel to be filled on one side of the lake and sold on the other.

Like many Israeli veterans he wears his kibbutz experience like a campaign medal. But unlike the others, he is restless, gregarious (seeking company rather than intimacy) and cosmopolitan. In the pre-state years he was the perfect liaison man: first between the Haganah political and military organization and the British CID (he could drink any British policeman under the table, a rare accomplishment for a Jew); then in Istanbul helping Holocaust survivors; later in the United States collecting weapons for the new state and as a pioneer of Israel's relations with the CIA. The details of his work during this period have never been told. His detractors maintain that this is because his role was a minor one, he himself because state secrets were involved.

When he returned to Israel from the United States, to serve as director-general of Ben Gurion's office in 1952, Kollek still avoided involvement in party politics. Among his other duties, he dealt with the radio and press, during the period when they were under much pressure from 'the Old Man' (Kollek still has an ambivalent relationship with the Hebrew press, which first spoiled, recently savaged

44

him); he reorganized the country's tourist industry and helped the restoration of historic sites like Caesaria and Masada. There is a famous story of how Ben Gurion, notoriously blind to the visual arts, ordered Kollek to take down a painting, at Israel's Tenth Anniversary Exhibition site, by one of the country's leading artists, Yosef Zaritsky, with the words 'Remove that scribble!' Kollek moved the painting to a less prominent place in the exhibition. Later, in 1967, Ben Gurion was to propose pulling down the medieval walls of Jerusalem, an idea rejected by Kollek and most others.

Kollek hosted visiting VIPs (including Pope Paul II in 1963), helped purchase the Dead Sea Scrolls, and arranged the facilities for the Eichmann trial (which he attended only once; he has never made political capital of his work during the Holocaust). When Ben Gurion broke with the old Labour Party, Mapai, in 1965, Kollek felt that out of loyalty he should leave too, and went out with him into the political wilderness. Kollek's role as majordomo to Israel's greatest leader had now come to an abrupt end. Ben Gurion himself, Kollek's admired mentor, was now on the fringes of Israeli politics: during the election campaign which followed, the man who had taken the decision to establish the State of Israel could be seen standing at windy street corners in Jerusalem, haranguing the small groups of passers-by who could not understand why the security mishap known as the 'Lavon Affair' had become a symbol of injustice and betrayal for 'the Old Man'.

Nothing in Kollek's previous career appeared to have suited him for the humdrum role of mayor of west Jerusalem. His predecessor, Mordechai Ish-Shalom, a Labour man, was by all accounts an excellent administrator who had established the main municipal services in the growing city and with its treasurer, Yosef Uzieli, straightened out the city's failing finances. But he had none of Kollek's personality. In Israel, where the founding generation of politicians cling to office into advanced old age, Kollek at fifty-five was one of Israel's young men. His major interest in Jerusalem, however, was not the municipality but the recently opened Israel Museum, which, as he put it later, was 'the only great cultural achievement of the State of Israel' (the Hebrew University was founded in 1925; and the Philharmonic Orchestra in 1936).

Kollek's campaign crackled with energy and ambition. Even in

1965 he was talking of Jerusalem as a potential 'world city' which needed another hundred thousand hotel beds, more great parks and theatres, and he suggested appealing to the outside world for help and reviving Sir Ronald Storrs' 'Pro Jerusalem' society – the genteel English embryo of the Jerusalem Foundation. Kollek put Ish-Shalom, with his solid record of having improved Jerusalem's sewers, in the shade, and harnessed the religious parties with promises of a wide post-election coalition. (He also promised that if he got a majority, he would change the electoral system entirely.) However, on the eve of the polls, he called off a public debate with Ish-Shalom. It might have indicated his total ignorance of municipal affairs.

As an outside runner for Ben Gurion's Rafi Party faction against the powerful party machine of Labour, Kollek did well. But he did not get his majority. His faction tied with that of Labour, which – in the national elections held simultaneously – was again returned to power.

Had Kollek been a conventional Labour man, he would not have become mayor. Until that time, no follower of Ben Gurion's had dared form a coalition with the right-wing Herut Party; it was an iron principle of Ben Gurion's that neither the Herut people nor the communists should join an Israeli coalition government. Herut, which had defied Ben Gurion's leadership during the pre-state period, had been outlawed; Ben Gurion had seized their arms and handed over those suspected of terrorist actions to the British – a policy in which he was assisted by his young lieutenants, including Kollek. But in 1965 Kollek decided to shrug off the past. He wanted the city leadership and he wanted it straight away. 'For garbage collection', he was to say later, 'it wasn't necessary to examine people's political credentials.'

Kollek made up his coalition with the religious parties and Herut, and flew off to America on museum business a few hours later.

His first year and a half as mayor were not distinguished. The city was much too small for Kollek, except at Christmas time, when he made the most of the ecumenical opportunities at the Mandelbaum Gate, handing out hot soup to Christian pilgrims and chatting with the commuting Patriarchs. He gallantly refused to move the municipality to a less exposed part of the city, on the grounds that working-class Jerusalemites living on the frontier had no such option. Meanwhile, as he later admitted, he was looking for an honourable way out of a job he found frustrating.

Kollek's moment came with the Six Day War. During this period he asserted his leadership both in the municipal and the political sense. In the disorder of the first few days after Israel's troops moved eastwards, even before street fighting had completely ceased, Kollek assured General Narkiss, the local military commander, that he could renew services throughout the city; he took emergency supplies to Arab civilians and within hours was cleaning the streets of rubble and corpses with the help of east Jerusalem's municipal workers, and linking the water lines between the two sides of the city, which had been severed in 1948. On 10 June he tore down the Moors Quarter and was already planning, with the City Council, to renovate the Old City.

During the 1967 battle, many Israeli soldiers' lives had been lost because the soldiers themselves were unfamiliar with the city's topography. Others died because of the government's decision not to shell the Old City directly for fear of destroying the Holy Places – all of which, save for the Western Wall, belonged to Christians and Moslems. Once the city was in Jewish hands, however, both the army and the municipality sent out demolition squads to destroy semi-derelict buildings which were either threatening to collapse or stood in the way of plans for the clearing of an open area round the Old City walls. The city had barely replaced windows in the Anglican Cathedral property when the army, working nearby, blew them out again. 'We are finding the peace more dangerous than the war,' remonstrated the Anglican archbishop.

No political instructions yet existed as to what was to be done regarding the civil administration of east Jerusalem; it was not until three weeks after the battles, on 29 June, that Israeli law was formally introduced into the area. The battle for Jerusalem had been fought between the Israeli and the Jordanian armies over the heads of the Palestinian civilians; the standing instructions of General Dayan, the Minister of Defence, were to allow the Arabs of the occupied territories to run their own municipal affairs.

During this interim period, Kollek had no desire to co-opt Arabs on to the City Council. In east Jerusalem, where the civilian administration was still in deep shock, the illusion prevailed briefly that despite the Israeli victory, the Arabs might retain autonomy over their municipal affairs. This was an illusion encouraged by Kollek when, on 21 June, he visited the east Jerusalem municipality, reminisced about mandatory times with the Arab mayor, Ruhi el Khatib, and expressed the hope that 'the two municipalities would function in friendship'. A week later, when Israeli law was imposed, the eastern City Council ceased to exist. At Kollek's urging, the deputy military commander summoned the Arab City Council to a meeting and read them an official order (in Hebrew) informing them that they were dismissed.

Kollek was to argue in later years that Arab councillors might have been co-opted on to the Jewish City Council but that the government had 'botched it up'. It was true that the government had authorized the Minister of the Interior to appoint additional members to the City Council from east Jerusalem and, in fact, instructed the Arabs to name candidates — which they refused to do. But according to Meron Benvenisti, one of Kollek's closest colleagues in the post-war municipality, all Kollek himself wanted at this stage was an 'advisory committee' and feared that admitting Arabs to the Council would merely have given them a platform for anti-Israeli propaganda. In any case, no Arab was consulted.

The irony of the situation was that for the next two decades, Kollek himself was to search for a formula which would allow the Arabs of the city, under Israeli sovereignty, self-government.

Teddy Kollek saw his 'world city' grow at an astounding pace between 1967 and 1979. By 1976, Jerusalem had become the largest city in the country, with 366,000 inhabitants — over 10 per cent of the total population of Israel, and outstripped Tel Aviv (calculated without its satellite towns). Bulldozers churned great swathes out of the hilltops, cranes swung perpetually over the city centre, and a new road shortened the distance between the coast and the capital from an hour and a half to fifty minutes. Real estate entrepreneurs rushed in with extravagant plans for business centres and skyscrapers, and all the big hotel chains set up their interchangeable caravanserai with piped music, skating rink foyers and boutiques selling Israeli export furs, leather coats and diamonds — goods for which there never had been much demand in shabby Jerusalem. Kollek enlarged the Jerusalem Book Fair, initiated by his predecessor Ish-Shalom, held in the

convention centre at the entrance to the city; created the Spring Festival, with shaven Japanese dancers hanging upside down from the
amphitheatre on Scopus dedicated by Weizmann and Balfour; and
encouraged Isaac Stern and Yitzhak Perlman to give master classes
at the new music centre. Leon Uris and Saul Bellow visited the now
famous Montefiore almshouse, Mishkenot Shaananim. Jerusalem, for
the first time, became an elegant place to visit. The Mayor toured
the world lobbying for the Foundation, and appearing, like Hitchcock
in his films, briefly at each event: hovering on the edges of happenings,
lowered on firemen's ladders, delivering ever briefer speeches, and
falling asleep regularly at celebrity concerts.

The city's gardeners had many different blueprints presented to
them at a rapid pace. Soon there was scarcely an intersection in west
Jerusalem without its little triangle of roses and oleander, or a new
housing project without a Foundation park with fibreglass slides and
adventure playgrounds. Between the Knesset and the nearest working-
class and middle-class districts (the 'Nachlaot' and the Wolfson
towers), the Sacher park, which provided picnic and sports areas
as well as the site of the Moroccan Jews' spring 'Maimouna' festival,
was installed. After the Dutch government moved its embassy from
Jerusalem, the Israel Netherlands Committee, a group set up in sympathy with Israel, sent a hundred thousand tulip bulbs each spring
to the Cultural Mile. Six hundred types of rose were planted in one
of the Foundation's gardens near the Prime Minister's Office, a display
to rival the Shah's rose park in Shiraz. The Mormons donated a
million dollars for a 'Spiritual Park' on the Mount of Olives. There
was even a garden for the blind in a district shared by Jews and
Arabs, with braille inscriptions describing the view. Hillsides were
decorated with sculptures by Calder and Lipschitz. All this in a city
where, barely a few years earlier, recent immigrants from Romania
and Algeria had come in from the suburbs to watch the first traffic
lights installed change colour; where, in the stuffy hall of the old
Edison Cinema, Daniel Barenboim had waited until the first showing
was over to play Beethoven sonatas, drowned during the *allegro con
moto* by the roar of bus engines outside; and where the only public
sculpture in the city was the 'Davidka', an aged mortar used in the
War of Independence.

In the Old City the stall owners had very rapidly recouped the losses sustained during the war because the Israelis had immediately invaded the markets and bought up everything in sight. The Old City was Jerusalem's biggest attraction for tourists, with its great churches and monasteries, its vaulted markets and packed bazaars, its tattoo parlours, fortune tellers and pinball machines. Soon the merchants were selling not only Bedouin carpets, hubble-bubble pipes, icons and mother of pearl crosses, but also stars of David, seven-branched candlesticks and T-shirts saying 'I came to Israel and all I got was this lousy T-shirt'. The grocers sold all the spices of Arabia; also Israeli tinned pineapple and matzos for Passover. The cognoscenti bought antiquities and Bethlehem embroidery at ridiculously low prices, and the others bought fake ancient oil-lamps, uncured sheep-skin coats that never lost their odour, and shoes that fell apart after the first wearing. But there was another aspect of the Old City which the tourists found less attractive.

There was a forest of television aerials over the domed roofs, corrugated iron awnings stretched over the shopfronts, and butchers' shops where the carcasses lay in tubs of water which was changed once a week. The odour of fur and flesh and open drains was everywhere, and there were piles of garbage at every corner.

Kollek took his municipal teams in and rallied the philanthropists around him. He planned the replacement of the television aerials by a central underground network and refaced the more prominent shopfronts. The butchers were ordered to install refrigerators. The Old City was provided with a regular water supply. Water had been piped in, under the Jordanians, only once or twice a week, and Jerusalem had relied chiefly on its cisterns and reservoirs. Now it was linked with the Israeli Water Carrier, which supplies almost all the city's needs.

The government had recommended only that the city maintain the existing (Jordanian) services. Kollek had different ideas. The problem was that no one had really anticipated what would happen when fresh water began rushing into pipes and tanks throughout the medieval city. There was tremendous pressure on the Turkish and partly Roman drainage system, five hundred years old and more. The ancient junctions sagged and split, and water began rising into the foundations of the houses in the lower lying parts of the Old City. The Holy Sepulchre was among the first buildings to be waterlogged and several monasteries and churches were flooded. The municipal engineers were forced to start a wholesale replacement of the drainage system; street after street was torn up and new pipes laid down. Shopkeepers lost customers and had to be compensated; work had to be halted on Moslem and Christian holidays; tourists had to climb over ditches and along planks to do their shopping.

This was not all. The digging and drilling had shaken those old buildings whose foundations were weak. Cracks appeared and houses began to lurch and subside. The municipal engineers returned to the attack. Millions of dollars were invested in the reinforcement of the city, including great injections of concrete into the Old City walls themselves, which were rotten with damp and had been crumbling for centuries.

The Via Dolorosa was partly relandscaped and repaved. At its starting point inside the Lion's Gate, the architect in charge had to carry out negotiations with the Moslem Wakf, which owns the surrounding land, and plans went back and forth to Amman in Jordan for approval. At the Ecce Homo arch, between the Third and Fourth Stations of the Cross, the installation of drains revealed ancient paving stones from the time of Christ which were raised into position, each stage of the work needing consultation with the Latins, the Greek Orthodox and the Moslem Wakf on whose property the area bordered.

Not all city improvements were equally welcome to the churches. The Franciscan fathers complained that tourists on the newly opened Ramparts Walk could look straight into their bedroom windows, and feared terrorists might toss bombs into their gardens. The city stationed guards on the walls. The Provost of the Lutheran church was displeased that in the nearby Jewish Quarter, the new Rooftop Promenade passed far too near the church; backpackers settled there to play their guitars and picnic, while hurrying Hassidim took short cuts to their seminaries in the Moslem Quarter over Lutheran property.

But these were minor problems compared with the pleasure taken both by churchmen and tourists in the newly salubrious public precincts of the Old City. The work done by the city, and by the East Jerusalem Development Company, a government organization which worked closely with Kollek's staff, encouraged both Christians and

Moslems to expand their own restoration and rebuilding programmes. Since 1948, almost all the repair work done in the city
had been concentrated on the Holy Sepulchre – in the past the victim
of earthquake (in 1927), flood and fire, and the great mosques on
the Temple Mount. Arab craftsmen have trained at Ravenna and
have restored both the mosaics in the cupola of the Al Aqsa mosque
and a small Mameluke temple near the Dome of the Rock. The huge
underground hall probably constructed by the Templar knights called
the Stables of Solomon, but which until recently looked more like
the Augean stables, has been cleaned, and Islamic monuments, tombs
and market-places elsewhere in the Moslem Quarter restored despite
the problems involved in working in areas crammed with shops and
residents. Today Kollek could not accuse the city's Arabs, as he did
several years ago via a Palestinian journalist at a Council meeting,
of failing to look after their own monuments.

Whatever the motivation – political, aesthetic or commercial –
the Old City, from being one of the world's most neglected historic
sites, has become, since 1967, the centre of intensive restoration.
Yet behind this impressive façade, Kollek's administration has faced
a host of problems which have constantly threatened his achievements
and his solutions, and have not always deflected criticism of his role
as an administrator. These are: the problem of the gap between the
level of services in the Jewish and Arab sectors; the problem of the
immense strain placed on municipal services by the construction of
the peripheral suburbs; opposition to development plans at the city
centre by the conservationist lobby; criticism of his increasingly intimate relations with the eastern churches. There are also signs that
there is something in the very nature of the city which resists moderni-
zation.

3

The View from City Hall

DURING THE EARLY YEARS after 1967, the chief complaint
of the Arab population was the level of Israeli taxation. 'This
is the way the Arabs feel the occupation,' said one of their
leaders, Anwar Nusseibeh, at the time. Today the main complaint
is that despite the fact that the Arabs pay their taxes, they do not
receive equal services. No one denies this. A recent report from the
City Treasurer's office described many Arab areas of the city as rural
pockets lacking paved roads, drainage, sewerage and telephones. The
proposed budget for improvements in the Arab sector, according to
this estimate, would cost about 40 per cent of Jerusalem's entire
municipal budget. Over half of this would have to be spent on infrastructure and the construction of more Arab schoolrooms. This indicates the scale of the problem Kollek faces, and the reason why,
when asked what his first priority would be if the government finally
granted him his development fund, he immediately responds: 'The
Arab sector.'

Where the government is concerned, however, the Arabs of Jerusalem, who are not citizens of the state, are clearly last on the list
of priorities. The Israeli Ministry of Housing, which between 1967
and 1986 built 34,000 of the 63,000 new homes for Jewish families
in the city, built or provided loans to help construct some four hundred
Arab houses. This, while the annual growth rate of Jerusalem Arabs,
where natural increase is concerned, was until recently far higher
than that of the Jews.

According to the latest survey carried out by the Institute for Jerusalem Studies, the Arab population now constitutes over 30 per cent
of the city's residents, or 140,000 souls. Yet, by its own choice, it
has no voice on the City Council. To participate in running the city,
leading Arabs in east Jerusalem argued publicly (and until last June
unanimously), would mean recognizing the legitimacy of Israeli rule.
Kollek has thus been forced into a paternalist role to which, ever
since 1967, he has sought an alternative.

Originally, Kollek hesitated between two solutions: one was to
co-opt leading figures in east Jerusalem on to the City Council; the

other, to establish a separate and autonomous municipal body which would enable the Jerusalem Arabs to look after their own roads, sanitation, education and health.

The first solution proved unworkable because of the Arab refusal. The second aroused Israeli opposition because of its political implications.

Kollek maintains that until the summer of 1969 he had hopes of recruiting Arab leaders on to the City Council. These were not, he says, to be token figures, straw men, but responsible leaders. However, in July 1969 a deranged Australian Christian tourist, Michael Rohan, bribed his way into the Al Aqsa mosque and set fire to the building. Except for the destruction of a thirteenth-century pulpit whose remains are still preserved in the Islamic Museum nearby, the physical damage to the mosque was reparable. The damage to Israel-Arab relations in the city was incalculable. Though the subsequent enquiry revealed that it was the negligence of the Moslem guards – the entire area being under Wakf supervision – which was to blame, in Jerusalem the origin of incidents is unimportant. What counts is what happens. The Moslems already knew that extremist religious and right-wing Jews resented Moslem control of the Temple Mount, and successive later attempts, during the 1980s, to breach the Mount by groups of Jewish fanatics proved that the entire area is terrifyingly vulnerable. If the fire in Al Aqsa was the real reason for Arab leaders not to sit on the City Council, there has been little subsequent reason for them to change their minds.

Three months before the fire, Kollek, speaking to the foreign press, had made an alternative, 'purely private' suggestion for Arab participation in municipal affairs. This was a proposal for a 'greater Jerusalem' stretching from Ramallah in the north to Bethlehem in the south, incorporating independent Arab and Israeli Jerusalems, with an Arab university in what would be an Arab capital. Plans for such an enlargement, says Kollek, had been found among the papers of the Jordanians left in Jerusalem.

The proposal has to be seen against the background of the period. Labour was in power and its leaders were toying with the idea of a 'territorial compromise' with Jordan. The so called 'Allon Plan' envisaged the return of much of the West Bank to Jordan, leaving only strategic hilltops and a strip of territory along the Jordan river in Israeli hands. In this context, there was discussion not only of a form of Palestinian autonomy but of a 'corridor' which might link Amman and the Islamic Noble Sanctuary (the Temple Mount) over which a Moslem (Wakf) flag might fly.

Such ideas had been current from shortly after the 1967 war. In 1968, the Israeli Foreign Ministry had commissioned Meron Benvenisti, Kollek's head of east Jerusalem affairs, to work out a proposal which was, according to the terms of reference, 'to ensure the unity of Jerusalem under our sovereignty, and at the same time to satisfy non-Israeli (especially Jordanian) interest'. Benvenisti suggested the creation of 'a single municipal county under dual sovereignty', a 'Greater Jerusalem' which would include united Jerusalem, under Israeli rule, and the rest of the non-annexed metropolitan area, under that of Jordan. This plan was later called the 'Borough Scheme', as it envisaged separate boroughs for the city on analogy with the Greater London Council.

The plan was leaked to the press, with numerous distortions, in 1971. Benvenisti himself was subjected to an unparalleled attack by the right wing, both in City Hall and in the Knesset. He was labelled a traitor and a defeatist, his life was threatened, and a right-wing Knesset member called for him to be put on trial. As Benvenisti put it, he 'became such a political liability' to Kollek that the Mayor was 'forced to abandon [him] until the storm passed'.

Yet, as already seen, Kollek had adopted Benvenisti's plan in the spring of 1969 (today Kollek says he had no prior knowledge of it whatsoever). A short time after his speech, the Mayor came under attack in the City Council, despite his protestations that his proposal could be merged with national policy. A month later, he promised to refrain from making any more 'political statements' of this kind. Nevertheless, Kollek was later to promote a version of Benvenisti's scheme as a decentralized municipal system which, he suggested, would be of benefit to both Jews and Arabs.

After the Yom Kippur War, when it looked as if the 'peace process' launched by the United States was to affect Jerusalem, Kollek once more revived the borough idea but this time with no suggestion of Arab sovereignty. In 1980 he even sent a team of senior officials to London to study whether its current system could be transplanted to Jerusalem. (The answer was no.) Today, Kollek says that the borough idea has become 'a code-word, on the right wing, for the redivision of the city'. The Jewish attitude to the idea of Arab representation in the running of this city remains ambivalent. In February 1987 Kollek said that he discouraged the idea when it was put to him by Arabs, on the grounds that the PLO would be gunning for any Arab candidate. 'I've warned the Arabs who want to join the municipality (i.e. on Kollek's own list) that it could cost them their lives. I had one experience, something I feel very guilty about. I organized a discussion between some Arabs and people from the *New York Times* and then it was published, and a man's name was mentioned, and afterwards he was killed. Perhaps there were other reasons for the murder – but I feel guilty.'

Arab participation could also be dangerous for the Mayor himself, in the political sense. Jerusalem is in many ways a less tolerant place today than it was in 1969.

Benvenisti was to return to City Hall, at Kollek's request, as Deputy Mayor in charge of planning, soon after the Yom Kippur War, and remained in office until 1978. But the Mayor and the man who had inspired so many of his ideas for Jewish-Arab coexistence in the city were, sadly, unable to work together after this date. Benvenisti has since then devoted himself to the study of the Palestinian-Israeli relationship and, as editor of a research project, with a report on affairs in the area, is one of the most articulate critics of Israeli settlement and policy in the West Bank.

When the compromise proposal of Kollek and Benvenisti failed, Kollek's coalition accepted the responsibility for Arab welfare in the city, with the Arabs as passive, if discontented, beneficiaries. But this arrangement rested on the assumption, on the Israeli side, that municipal affairs and national politics could be kept separate indefinitely. In June 1987 a dramatic statement by a leading Palestinian figure in east Jerusalem challenged this belief openly for the first time.

On the eve of the twentieth anniversary of the Six Day War, speaking at a meeting between the Palestinian press and members of the foreign press corps, Hanna Siniora, editor of the *Al Fajr* newspaper, announced that he intended to head a Palestinian list for the November 1988 municipal elections. The statement was revolutionary in a number of senses. For the first time, a Jerusalem Palestinian was calling on his people to participate as of right in an Israeli administrative body, and to share the responsibility for running the city.

Siniora's moves, triggered by the current political stalemate, caused consternation both in Israeli and Palestinian circles. Both Kollek and his main rival in the Likud, Reuven Rivlin, welcomed Siniora's statement as an indication that a Palestinian was prepared to recognize Israel's sovereignty and participate in an Israeli-run municipality. Both men ignored Siniora's explanatory statement: 'This does not mean we relinquish sovereignty over east Jerusalem. I believe Jerusalem should be an undivided city with dual sovereignty, the capital of both a Palestinian state and of Israel.'

Siniora also stated that he would welcome a separate Arab administrative area in east Jerusalem: in effect the first revival of the 'borough' idea since 1980, but in a clear political context.

Such statements could not go unchallenged. Right-wing members of the Knesset immediately called for moves to outlaw any supporters of the PLO (*Al Fajr* supports the mainstream Fatah faction led by Yasser Arafat) standing for election to the municipality. Meanwhile, almost all leading Palestinians, both in Jerusalem and the West Bank, and spokesmen of all factions of the PLO, as well as pro-Jordanian newspapers, condemned Siniora's initiative.

Siniora himself said he had anticipated the criticism. He insisted that it would take time for both Israelis and Palestinians to digest this idea. Siniora's proposal is more a reminder, to Israelis, that two peoples inhabit Jerusalem than a plan that – at present – seems likely to win the necessary support. Its implications are nevertheless important.

There are currently 70,000 potential Arab voters for local elections in Jerusalem. Siniora believed that he could rally about half of these behind an Arab list and win between four and six places in the thirty-one-man municipal council, thus achieving a pivotal role in city politics. Theoretically at least such an Arab list could siphon off the two critical seats in Kollek's municipal faction currently provided by Arab voters.

Kollek himself has expressed great scepticism both as to the practical worth of Siniora's proposal and as to Siniora's own importance in the Palestinian community. In Kollek's view, the Palestinians are likely to continue to reject participation in the municipal council, especially in view of the proven achievements of his own faction on the Arabs' behalf.

In principle, however, there is nothing in the legislative sense to prevent an Arab list from appearing at some time in the future, or to prevent Palestinian nationalists from using the municipal council not only to improve conditions in east Jerusalem, but also as a platform for political change. Thus the Israeli right wing has already called for preventive legislation. Thus, too, many liberal Israelis have welcomed Siniora's statement as a reminder that, given the demographic facts and without a new political initiative, Israel is headed either for a bi-national state, or might become a Jewish state which would be forced to deny its Arab citizens their basic rights.

Where the record of Arab employees in the municipality since 1967 is concerned, the results are not encouraging. The city took the lead in employing most of the ex-Jordanian municipal workers in 1967. It was prepared to extend special contracts to the Arabs and to underwrite their pension funds. Nevertheless, over twenty years, no east Jerusalem Arab has been appointed head of a municipal department. The highest ranking east Jerusalem Arab official in the city's employ is the aide to the City General Manager.

The official explanation for this situation is that no qualified personnel — for instance in the engineering section — have applied. But one of the most talented administrators ever to work for the city believes that the reason is that senior Jewish officials will not agree to work under an Arab in the city administration.

Many of the municipal jobs demand a knowledge of Arabic, and day-to-day work in Arab districts is carried out, in many cases, by some of the Israeli Arabs resident in the city.

Several thousand Israeli Arabs, formerly residents of towns and villages under Israeli rule (only a handful had remained in west Jerusalem), today live in reunified Jerusalem. Many are students and others from Arab centres in the Galilee and the part of the central plain called the Little Triangle. These are Arabs with Israeli citizenship, the right to vote, and a much greater familiarity with the Israeli welfare state and its bureaucracy than most Arabs who have lived under Israeli rule only since 1967. Many students, particularly in the law faculty of the Hebrew University, study on Mount Scopus. In recent years some Arab graduates of Israeli universities have found employment in Jerusalem and in the municipality. But their role is perhaps the most delicate of all. They work for fellow Arabs (some would call them fellow Palestinians) who have no political rights and regard themselves as 'under occupation', and some of whom regard the Israeli Arabs as traitors to the Palestinian cause. On the one hand, the Israeli Arabs feel that their particular task is to improve local conditions and instruct east Jerusalem Arabs as to their civic rights; on the other, many share the resentment and bitterness of the east Jerusalem population at their political deprivation.

Pending political change or the evolution of an independent Arab party, Kollek is stuck with his paternalist role. As the government is so reluctant to divert funds to the Arab sector of the city, Kollek has sought what he calls 'palliatives', chief among them the funds available via his Foundation, in which an entire separate department deals with east Jerusalem. The most impressive Foundation project for the Arabs is the Sheikh Jarrah Health Centre. Built by the Foundation, it was rented to the Israeli trades union health fund, the Histadrut Kupat Holim, for $50,000 a year, money fed back into the clinic. The centre, praised even by the most militant of Palestinian leaders in east Jerusalem, serves forty thousand people, about a third of the total population in Arab districts, and compares favourably with similar facilities in other parts of the country; it is staffed by Arab doctors and nurses. Because it is hard to raise money from Jewish donors for the Jerusalem Arabs, Kollek has found supporters in West Germany, like Axel Springer and Frieder Burda, and others among Protestant groups in the United States. Many of the Foundation projects in east Jerusalem have been set up discreetly, without the fanfare which accompanies the inauguration of parks and community centres in Jewish districts. One community centre, which caters for twenty thousand people and is run by an Israeli Arab social worker, functions without the famous Foundation plaque or indeed any sign that it is funded and maintained by a Jewish organization. This, despite the fact that it is fully documented in brochures produced by the Foundation.

At the end of October 1986, the head of the Urban Improvement Department in the municipality, Yoel Marinov, paid a visit to a group of tenants in Fig Tree Road, in the Jerusalem suburb of Gilo. They wanted the city to help clear up the waste lots and neglected patches of land beyond their small, carefully tended oasis. The Ministry of Housing builds, lays out the surrounding area and leaves; the city is responsible for maintenance.

Gilo is the southernmost of the vast peripheral suburbs built, by government fiat, for thirty thousand people on a series of hilltops between Bethlehem and Jerusalem. Two huge crescents of apartment blocks cap the hills, among which a few of the original fig and almond trees survive. Fig Tree Road is one of the few intimate corners of a suburb which is notably deficient in human touches, a dormitory laid out by committees of architects and engineers who were rarely to meet the people who lived there. Gilo, with its vast retaining walls, its near empty six-lane highways, its huge inner courtyards between extravagant superblocks, was left with gardening and maintenance costs beyond the tenants' resources, inadequate health and education facilities, and a sense of isolation from the city centre. The tenants of Fig Tree Road tried to do something about it. They hired a team of gardeners at their own expense, decorated the façades of their buildings with herbaceous borders and window-boxes, and planted flower-beds at the centre of the secluded square at the end of the road. In the very centre of these flower-beds were two enormous blue iron skips.

The presence of the skips was only one of the tenants' grievances, but it is an example of the municipal dilemma posed by maintenance of the peripheral suburbs. Gilo is miles from the centre; the pick-up points for garbage have to be reduced to the minimum, and the skips have grown steadily fewer, and larger. The visit of the head of a department followed a number of different appeals to different authorities, most of which were unanswered; the meeting was eventually arranged through the recently formed neighbourhood committee, one of several set up to help tenants caught in what sociologists define as a situation of 'hostile dependence' on central and local authorities.

When the government first began building the outer suburbs, there were fears that Jews would not want to live in these new districts, cut off as they were from west Jerusalem by intervening Arab districts. But the new neighbourhoods provided public housing of a standard previously unknown in the capital, and there was soon a rush to register for the newly allocated flats. Today about 100,000 people, or nearly one-third of the Jewish population of Jerusalem, live in these districts – a cordon previously intended to protect Jerusalem from physical assault by Arab armies, but which is now seen as preventing the spread of the surrounding Arab population towards the Jewish capital.

The price, for the municipality, was high. When the first ring of suburbs to the north-east was built, the criteria for density and height laid down by the city's planners were ignored by the Ministry of Housing, which did the actual building. When the municipal officials, inspecting French Hill, complained, they were told that they were standing in the way of national priorities. Kollek himself objected to the construction of Gilo. In 1976 he appealed to the Labour government to block the project, arguing that basic services had not even been ensured in one suburb before another was started. If Gilo was intended to protect Jerusalem's southern approaches, he wrote to the Labour minister Israel Galili, there was a nearby Israeli field school which, if necessary, could be enlarged and fortified. Kollek was overruled.

The new suburbs, by providing public housing only on the periphery, contributed to an exodus from the centre, where land prices rose astronomically. They broke up the carefully integrated pattern of Jerusalem schools, which by the 1960s had ensured equal opportunities for the children of both the veteran and immigrant Jewish populations, and which Kollek had fought for against middle-class opposition. The government allocated vast sums to the infrastructure of the suburbs, but little to the municipality to build new community centres, schools and clinics. The public housing is of a high standard; the villa sections luxurious; but most of the suburbs suffer from their remoteness from central facilities and their design, which spreads them out across the hilltops like great walls. Even after more than a decade, the suburbs have not managed to establish a life of their own; during the day, most of them are deserted save for mothers of small children and old people. Very few have local restaurants, there are no local cinemas or places of entertainment, and transport into the centre is infrequent during the day and stops completely between mid afternoon on Friday and Saturday night. Kollek says of Gilo: 'It will take two generations to correct all the errors of planning.' That correction is now being undertaken by the city, with community centres and sports grounds being constructed under its own supervision.

Kollek has also opposed, without success, the setting up of Jewish satellite towns all round Jerusalem but *outside* the municipal borders – most of them in the West Bank but one, Mevasseret Zion, a prestige commuter village on the way to Tel Aviv. The satellite towns in the West Bank – Maalei Adumim, on the road to Jericho; Efrata; Betar and Givat Ze'ev (not to be confused with the Jerusalem suburb of Pisgat Ze'ev, both called after the Herut leader Jabotinsky) – have drawn off thousands of potential taxpayers from Jerusalem as well as potential Jerusalemites from the coastal areas. The cost of buying houses and flats in these satellites, whose tenants are almost all commuters from the larger cities, is seven times less than that of accommodation in the capital. Kollek argues that this bait is possible because the Israel Lands Authority, which expropriated and sells the land, has kept its value artificially low, while the actual cost of supplying roads, electricity and water to the satellites is in fact extremely high, to the taxpayers' cost and also to the detriment of the municipal budget obtained from the government. Kollek was initially promised that the satellites would be built to provide homes for new immigrants, but in fact 98 per cent of the inhabitants of Maalei Adumim are ex-Jerusalemites.

Kollek's opposition has availed him little. Maalei Adumim was originally built because Moshe Dayan wanted an obstacle to Jordanian tanks on the way from the river to Jerusalem. The more recent expansion of this satellite, and the building of others, are right-wing policy carried out by the Herut-controlled Ministry of Housing, to which Labour opposition has been but feeble.

Jerusalem after 1967 had two separate development systems, one public and dominated by the Ministry of Housing, and one private, with Kollek courting every likely investor he could find to contribute to hotels, office buildings and the development of shopping centres. The western business centre of Jerusalem was largely in the hands of a few old Jerusalem families who had neither the wish nor the ability to develop their properties. Hence the anomaly that in central Jerusalem there are vacant lots behind hoardings which are filled with water in winter and rubbish in summer, and also the fact that foreign donors provide most funds for current development. The growing public lobby of those concerned for Jerusalem's traditional qualities protested not only against a handful of high-rise buildings, most of the permits for which had been allotted before 1967, but also against a number of later, even more ambitious, projects. One of them, Arthur Kutcher, wrote a book condemning government and city destruction of the sensitive area surrounding the Old City. Kollek's critics argued that he had no time for planners or for anything that came between him and his commitments to investors.

Kollek denies these criticisms fiercely. He asserts that he was against the ambitious road scheme condemned by the Jerusalem Committee from the outset, that soon after 1967 he realized, while on a tour of the city with the architect Mathias Goeritz, that high-rise buildings were unsuited to Jerusalem, that the city managed to cut down plans for the Jerusalem Sheraton Hotel by four storeys, and would have bought out the high-rise Hamashbir department store investors, had this been within its power financially.

Critics argue that Kollek refused the plea by the head of a government company to buy out the Fast Hotel investor on the gounds that he had given his word. The same thing, they say, happened over the building of the Plaza Hotel in one of the most sensitive open spaces facing the Old City walls, and clearly visible from the Mount of Olives. The head of the newly founded Council for a Beautiful Israel, the late writer Yehuda Haezrachi, suggested that bonds be issued for the redemption of the site by the public, which would buy out the investor. Kollek refused. His explanation is that the Finance Minister, Pinhas Sapir, had already turned down a proposal by the mayor to sell Jerusalem Bonds for between $12 and $30 million for the development of the city, to which foreign banks had already agreed in principle. Sapir argued that the government did not have the dollar reserves for repayment of income on the bonds, and was opposed to independent city financing. Kollek maintains that the rift with the environmentalists in the city began when they organized demonstrations of six- and seven-year-old children who were sent into the Omariya olive grove (where the Liberty Bell Garden now lies) to plant wild flowers in protest against the proposed erection of seven high-rise buildings. The plans for these buildings, according to Kollek, had already been rejected by the city.

But the most significant clash between Kollek and his environmentalist opponents in the city was over the Mamilla project, the thirty-acre site west of the Citadel.

Despite the linking of the basic infrastructure of the two parts of Jerusalem, there were, and still are, two open rents in the body of the city. One is the 'Seam' area running from the northern suburbs to the Old City walls, previously part of no man's land. The other is the Mamilla district between the Old City walls and the western commercial centre, called after what had been the smartest shopping street in mandate times.

It seemed to Kollek, soon after 1967, that if he could develop that particular patch of ground, he would be able to point to the physical reunification of Jewish and Arab Jerusalem.

Just at this time, a young architect named Moshe Safdie, who had grown up in Israel but now lived in Canada, took Jerusalem by storm. Safdie had made his name abroad with the precast, 'instant beehive' Habitat complex at the Montreal Expo of 1967. This was visited by seven million people and heralded as a breakthrough in twentieth-century architecture. Safdie arrived in Israel with a quiverful of new ideas: exciting substitutes for the drab, unimaginative public housing complexes of the 1950s, plans for a refugee city on the banks of the Jordan which would hasten the peace process, and a commitment to the idea that the Arabs and Jews of Jerusalem could be brought closer by intelligent urban design. Energetic, optimistic and unconventional, he won Kollek's support immediately. A public company, Carta, in which the municipality had only a minority interest, was set up to rebuild the Mamilla area, and Safdie was commissioned to produce a design.

Safdie's plan was probably the most ambitious project designed for the city since Roman times, though oddly enough it reflected not so much a compromise between Western and oriental styles, as a synthesis of a number of currently popular American innovations. It involved the restructuring of the whole area, with underground tunnels and parking lots to avoid blocking the Old City walls, open terraces, air-conditioned shopping malls and large residential blocks. But from the Yom Kippur War onwards, the opponents to the scheme grew daily, headed by Meron Benvenisti, now back in the municipality and head of planning. The plan was attacked as far too expensive and ambitious for Jerusalem. It went from hand to hand, was modified, cut back, redesigned, and provided a *casus belli* for some of the most vicious power struggles ever to be waged inside the municipality. Safdie, undeterred, continued to design other projects in the city. The Mamilla project confirmed Kollek in his dislike of the environmentalist lobby, which he was henceforth to attack without respite. The battle for Mamilla was to continue for years. In 1982, when the Beautiful Israel people, uninvited, took their complaints to the Jerusalem Committee, Kollek, who arrived for the session with an armful of 'Let's be tolerant' stickers, showed them the door.

During the 1970s there was already a consensus in Jerusalem that central Jerusalem was to be redeveloped modestly, by restoring some of the late nineteenth- and early twentieth-century quarters which had been neglected, and not by planting forests of skyscrapers. When Kollek took his new City Engineer, Amnon Niv, round the city for the first time – driving down one-way streets in the wrong direction and twice denting his Fiat 131 – he explained to him that only small changes were possible.

Niv periodically meets Kollek to review planning problems in the city. A Tel Aviv architect with a private practice, he has spent the last ten years as the City Engineer (in essence chief planner) and has finally laid down the zoning guidelines for every part of the city. Niv likes to describe a Jerusalem in which, for the first time in history, highways will run on an east–west bias through the city, linking Jordan – in a future, peaceful era – with the coast. In the northern part of the city, where the last land reserves are situated, Jews are to be housed to the east, Arabs to the west of the main highway – a reversal of the traditional pattern. And, Niv explains, the 'Seam' area, which runs south past Ammunition Hill to the Damascus Gate, can become the place where for practical reasons, and shared commercial interests, Jews and Arabs can come together. As a broad outline it is impressive. The detail indicates how far the vision still is from realization. The blueprint only becomes a legal, binding outline in small stages, handed from the local to the district planning offices for endorsement. There are battles every inch of the way.

While Kollek does not have the time to familiarize himself with every detail of the city's planning, he generally accepts the expert advice of his subordinates. As Niv and Kollek discuss the northern suburbs, two problems recur: if orthodox Jews are settled in large numbers near main roads, they will sooner or later try to block Sabbath traffic; and government planners disagree with the city's estimates of Arab housing needs.

Kollek, glancing at the map, asks why another east–west road can not be planned, linking two secular housing neighbourhoods.

'Teddy, there's a deep valley just there, it isn't possible,' puts in a young aide.

Niv briefs Kollek on plans for Wadi Joz, the great eastern valley beneath the slopes of Mount Scopus, now a garage and industrial area and a total eyesore. 'Why not evacuate the workshops and build Arab housing there?'

'Teddy,' says Niv patiently, 'the problem isn't just the evacuation, it's the compensation.' He explains the difficulties of locating owners and redistributing land. His idea is to offer groups of Arab landowners favourable building conditions, special mortgages, if they will merge their individual plots for a common project. Where the main rehousing project for Arabs to the north is concerned, Niv has been arguing for months with the District Planning Committee over the optimal number of housing units needed for the city's Arabs. The city says fifteen thousand, the Committee six thousand. In the end the city compromises on ten thousand units, anxious to release at least some of the permits applied for by Arab builders which have been piling up in the Engineer's office for months, even years.

Niv is one of the toughest critics of the Ministry of Housing's giant suburbs, and he and Kollek discuss how to bring back at least some of Jerusalem's younger population to the city centre, where even the older residential districts are becoming office areas. Niv explains that part of the difficulty is that young couples do not want to live among office buildings. Kollek nods: 'I have an elderly relation who has an apartment in a block where she is completely surrounded by offices; at night the whole place is deserted, old people are afraid to live there.' Issues are always clearer to Kollek when he can personalize them; he does not like abstracts. Niv argues that the actual needs of Jerusalem, the laws of supply and demand, have never been related to city planning.

The imbalance between the ambitious restoration plans and expansion of the city, and the constant problem of financing its basic services, is made even clearer at an emergency meeting a few days later, when Niv and Kollek talk with the heads of several municipal departments about the chronic shortage of classrooms in elementary schools throughout the city – and particularly in the new suburbs.

In 1985, for the first time since the period of peak immigration in the 1950s, there was a problem with school accommodation. By 1986, in order to prevent a recurrence of the problem, the head of the Education Department, Michael Gal, told the meeting of the need for temporary buildings. The city is short of thirty-three classrooms, which are needed for over a thousand children. (One of those present asks about the Arab sector, where the problem is even more desperate – 200 out of 540 classes study in improvised accommodation; but this question is postponed for separate discussion.) The officials argue about whether to put up prefabricated structures, cubes faced with stone, or flimsier metal shacks; and whether there is any way that such buildings can be legitimized in planning terms. The City Treasurer, Uzi Wechsler, is for the shacks, not only because they are cheaper but because 'elegant' temporary buildings have a way of becoming permanent. It is suggested that the buildings are erected without permits.

Niv opposes the temporary solution. 'With or without permits,' he says, 'it's my business.' By putting up temporary structures of any kind the city will be infringing the planning law organized finally after years of struggle.

'It's *our* law, let's change it,' fumes Kollek. 'It's not the Czar's law, I don't understand the objection. We don't provide extra classrooms for the Arabs, we turn them against us, but we can't break a silly law.' One of the deputy mayors warns Kollek that the temporary buildings will not get planning permission from the District Committee. Another suggests that the municipality go public on the issue, showing what happens when the government refuses to fork out the necessary funds to build new schools.

Niv is disturbed that a new precedent is being created: 'We can't afford to go back to putting up temporary, illegal buildings.' Kollek wants the matter disposed of quickly; precedents, permissions – all this does not interest him. What is vital to him is that the lack of schoolrooms is more damaging than building temporary quarters.

'Teddy's uninterested in the long term,' says a senior government official who worked closely with him for over twenty years. 'It's the short term that counts, for three reasons. He belongs to the generation which improvised everything they did, worked from scratch. He learned his trade at the kibbutz, at Ein Gev. You did what was possible and forgot about the rest. Secondly, there's his age: he can't look too far ahead. Thirdly, his main relationships are with his donors. It's a short-term association.'

Kollek says: 'I am sorry that we are not a rich city, and that our main relationship is with donors. The restoration of historical and religious sites has international importance, just as equalizing social services between Jews and Arabs is vital. Thus the Health Centre is a great boon. The difference between language, nationality and religion is quite enough, and if social services are not equal, it is too much to bear. This is the reason for the Jerusalem Foundation – and it is immoral that other cities should now be copying us [a reference to the fact that Tel Aviv's Mayor Lahat, head of a wealthy city, has also set up a competing Foundation]. The Foundation should be given up in a decade or so, we should be able to do without it, and I say this to the donors, I'm quite frank with them. The university and the Museum will continue to benefit from donations, but I don't think the Foundation will continue.'

The contrast between the ambitious and permanent, and the modest and 'temporary', is also characteristic of Jerusalem's cultural life. On the one hand there is the splendid Jerusalem Theatre, the Museum, the community centres put up by the Foundation, the Spring Festival and the celebrity performances at the Sultan's Pool. On the other, complain senior officials in the city, 'The Jerusalem Foundation has taken all the cultural activities out of the hands of the city and left it with the garbage.' Kollek dismisses this argument out of hand. He says that if the city had taken part in running these institutions, politics would inevitably have interfered. The city still controls public libraries, the Open University and community centres, as well as running the celebrations on Independence Day.

Alternative Jerusalem is therefore, quite literally, underground. The municipality, with no funds for local entertainments or cultural premises, took another look at the only public indoor spaces not in constant use – the shelters. From 1948 the city had built solid shelters against shelling and air raids; shelters must be built by law in all new buildings. It is only in the Old City that the perennially suspicious Arab owners are reluctant to have suitable rooms re-inforced against possible attack.

But save for a few days in 1967, and during practice sessions in schools, the shelters are never used and badly maintained. From 1977 it was decided that the State Lottery organization, Mifal HaPayis, would finance their renovation for use as synagogues, clubs, art and music schools, and local centres. The rent was low, the premises were equipped – as they had to be by law – with electricity and water, and the only condition for their occupation was that the tenants should be prepared to evacuate them, if necessary, within two hours.

Today about half of the two hundred and fifty shelters in Jerusalem's larger buildings are used for creative workshops, pocket theatres, ballet classes, even clubs for autistic children and old people. Most of the activity in the shelters is financed by the Jerusalem Foundation.

'I'm the only mayor in the world', Kollek says confidently 'who attends three midnight masses every Christmas' – that is, the Latin, Greek Orthodox and Armenian rites which take place at different times between December and January. His attendance is by special invitation; protocol does not dictate his presence, as it does that of the rather bored senior military personnel – government representatives – who fill the front rows of the Church of the Nativity at Bethlehem. Kollek relishes the ceremonies and returns the compliments. His Christian Affairs Advisor, Noemi Teasdale, keeps him up to date on the name days of the Eastern Patriarchs. Kollek staged an exhibition of Armenian art at the Israel Museum in 1969, persuaded the Greek Orthodox to open the Monastery of the Cross, with its gardens and chapels, to the public in 1986, and has encouraged the study of Aramaic in the schools of the Syrian Orthodox. Henry Kissinger and Gerald Ford have accompanied him to dinner with the Patriarch. But there is more to Kollek's relations with the churches than sampling potent liqueurs and admiring collections of antiquities.

Kollek's objectives are overtly political. The Israeli authorities all want to make it clear to the outside world not only that Israel maintains freedom of worship and is scrupulous in its protection of the

Christian Holy Places, but that the situation of the Christian communities under Israel is demonstrably better than it was during King Hussein's regime. Israel abolished the Jordanian laws which prevented the churches from buying property and building churches, and made the study of the passages from the Koran part of the curriculum of church schools. Kollek has even encouraged the founding of a Catholic university in Bethlehem in the West Bank. He has been not only directly responsible for Christian welfare in the day-to-day problems of maintenance and development; he has also rushed in to help when hooligans and fanatics attacked church property. In 1979–80 there was a series of cases of arson and vandalism: the Dormition Church on Mount Zion, a Catholic site; a Baptist church (burned down), the Protestant Bible Society shop and the Franciscan Christian Information Centre were all damaged. A formal protest was made by representatives of the churches to the Israeli Foreign Ministry; to their disappointment, instead of a public statement of concern by the Prime Minister (at that time Menachem Begin), they were merely handed a letter saying that he deplored the incidents. The police investigated and the offenders were punished. The Franciscan Custos, says Kollek, made use of the incidents to launch an anti-Israel campaign in the international Catholic press and, when the offenders were caught, Israel was not thanked. But it was Kollek who had taken the immediate action the churches wanted: he offered to repair the damage – where possible – at the city's expense. Kollek also installed bright street lighting to deter vandals.

It is Kollek, too, who has publicly acknowledged the Christian services from which Jews also benefit in Jerusalem. The Jerusalem Foundation has contributed to the Catholic St Louis Hospital – a hospice for the terminally ill which takes many Jewish patients – and made the director of the St Vincent de Paul home for handicapped children, Mère Claire Bernès, an honorary citizen of the city. Many of the children in this institution come from orthodox families.

The churches, most of whose property is in the Old City, have also obviously profited from the rehabilitation of the area and enjoyed priority where repair and maintenance work are concerned. Where they and Kollek have fallen out is over taxation. Here, as in so many aspects of life in the city, the situation in east Jerusalem is riddled with anomalies.

The city officially exempts the churches from two-thirds of the *arnona* (city rates). A service charge amounting to about a third of normal taxes was paid by the Christian institutions in west Jerusalem before 1967, for garbage collection and maintenance. East Jerusalem, however, previously paid no taxes to Jordan and continues to deny Israel's right to impose them. (Actual church buildings, like synagogues, mosques and schools, are exempt from taxation; but monasteries, hospices, offices and so on are not.) The Latin church has a particular grievance: it maintains that Israel has flagrantly ignored the obligations incurred when France and Italy, who own most of the Latin property in the city, recognized Israel in 1947. Part of the UN partition agreement under which Israel obtained this recognition guaranteed the continuation of tax exemptions practised by previous regimes. The municipality claims the one-third payment, but does not enforce it. The formal debts are now astronomical: and should the churches wish to sell their property (usually to one another) the sale theoretically cannot be registered until the debts are settled.

This may not seem a major problem (for the city would undoubtedly compromise in any final settlement), but it relates to the all-important question of the overall status of the churches in Jerusalem and in all the Holy Land, which is still undefined, unsatisfactory and a potential cause of conflict between the churches themselves, and between the churches and Israel. All the churches want some kind of recognized, independent status, not just a promise of free access to the Holy Places and a separate classification for bureaucrats in the Ministry of Religious Affairs – which is what they have at present. Instead of enjoying a blanket exemption from customs duties, for instance, the duties are charged, the churches apply to the Ministry, and the Ministry (if it agrees) pays the duty on the churches' behalf. So exemption depends on ministerial approval and the state of the Ministry's budget. City policy, says Kollek, is to protest against the present situation. But the churches are uneasily aware that the present situation leaves them open to pressures, both where taxation is concerned and when they have to apply for licences for building work and expansion.

When Cardinal O'Connor visited Israel in January 1987, Kollek complained: 'I have two thousand houses in the capital which don't

pay taxes, and I don't know why.' Kollek was referring to all the
historic and religious buildings in the city – synagogues, mosques
and churches – exempt from taxes. But one of the Catholic churchmen
present said it made them apprehensive. For the Mayor has never
made a secret of the fact that he regards himself as justified, in all
his relations with the churches, as acting not as a neutral administrator, but in what he regards as Israel's best interests. And the record
indicates that it is the relationship with the locally more powerful
Greek Orthodox church which, over the years, has proved of the
greatest interest to the Mayor.

The Greek Orthodox and the Armenian churches both owned valu-
able property in west Jerusalem and in the area to the west of the
Old City walls and, long before 1967, had proved willing to lease
large areas to Israel. Some of this land was originally leased to the
Jewish National Fund and used for parks, but was later re-zoned
for building and development. After 1967 much of the area fell within
Kollek's 'Cultural Mile' and while its value rose rapidly, the Israeli
currency depreciated in value. In 1977 the Greek Patriarchate even
went to court over its terms of lease with the Jewish National Fund,
but matters were always settled to the Greeks' satisfaction. The church
was later allowed to build, in this area and together with an Israeli
entrepreneur, a luxury apartment building. The Greek Orthodox
church received $5 million for a 140-year lease and building rights
on the plot, which covered a little under fifteen acres. Elsewhere,
too, both the municipal planners and the District Planning Committee
made generous acknowledgement of the Greeks' contribution to the
development of the city when considering the church's various plans
for expansion of its property in the Old City.

Kollek's relations with the Catholics were more chequered. All
their dealings with the Mayor were referred to the Vatican, which
was far more resistant than the Eastern churches to Kollek's efforts
to bring them into his grand plan for a new Jerusalem. The *Osservatore Romano* continually attacked Israel's building policy in the city
and only recently acknowledged the Old City renovations and praised
the restoration work in the Via Dolorosa.

While the local Catholic leaders – the Custos of the Franciscans,
who looks after the Holy Places, the Latin Patriarch who heads
the Catholic community, and the Apostolic Delegate, the Vatican

envoy – thanked Kollek politely for his efforts, they did not do so publicly.

It was not Vatican policy to lease church land, still less that in east Jerusalem, and despite Kollek's continuing efforts, it was not until the late 1970s that the Patriarchate and the Custos agreed to allow the city to develop a strip of land between the New and Damascus Gates, as part of the park surrounding the walls, and to lease land for a park in the French Hill area – after they had steadily failed to get a permit to build there. Despite the absence of diplomatic relations with the Vatican, Israeli officials had visited the Supreme Pontiff and Kollek was pleased when he received intimation, in May 1978, that the request for an audience with Pope Paul VI by the Mayor of Jerusalem would be welcomed. The time, however, was out of joint. The Christian militias in Lebanon were at each others' throats. Israel's anti-PLO campaign in Lebanon, 'Operation Litani', launched in March 1978, though backed by the Lebanese Maronites had not improved Israel's standing with the Catholic church. Further intimations were received that the visit might be better postponed until a more appropriate moment. Paul VI died in August of that year, and the historic meeting has still not taken place.

Then there was the incident of the Notre Dame hospice. This is the most prominent of Catholic hospices in the city, a rambling, shell-pocked building with a giant statue of the Virgin and Child on the roof, which faces the New Gate and overlooks the open fields between west and east Jerusalem. The building was quietly sold, without Vatican approval, by the Assumptionist order which owned it to the Hebrew University, just after the Six Day War. Two years later, the Apostolic delegate approached Kollek with a request from the Vatican: with the approval of the then Prime Minister, Golda Meir, and the Ministry of Justice, the building was returned to the Vatican for its sale price, though real estate values had risen four times meanwhile.

The building was restored and became, to all intents and purposes, a luxury hotel for Catholic pilgrims with a French restaurant said to be the best – and most expensive – in the city. Kollek decided to charge full rates to the building as a hotel, and a full-scale row developed between the city and the hospice administrator, Monsignor Richard Mathes. Eventually, a compromise was reached, since the other Catholic leaders in the city took Kollek's part.

Long before this incident, however – which took place in 1986 – it was clear that Kollek's view of Israel's interests was leading him into an increasingly intimate relationship with the Eastern churches, and not all government officials approved. As early as 1974, Kollek was proposing to the then Prime Minister, Yitzhak Rabin, that Israel revise its traditional preoccupation with the Vatican and pay more attention to the Eastern churches. But it was not until after 1977 that he found his views shared in high places. With Moshe Dayan as Foreign Minister in Menachem Begin's government, Kollek had a powerful supporter of his view that the Eastern churches were worth cultivating; moreover, he found himself freer to decide policy in Jerusalem since Begin had appointed, as senior officials in the Ministry of Religious Affairs, orthodox Jews whose views on the subject of the churches were more or less those expressed in a recent Council meeting by the Agudat Israel's Rabbi Leiserson. Leiserson, when apprised of plans to issue a permit to the Greek Orthodox to build a college in east Jerusalem, asked whether this might not be used as a centre for conversionist activities. When Kollek told him that he clearly did not know the difference between a Protestant Mission and a Greek Orthodox seminary, Leiserson retorted: 'I'm proud of my ignorance about the churches.'

With Dayan's tacit approval, between 1977 and 1981, policy towards the churches in the city was largely decided by Kollek, with, as his advisor, Raphael Levy, the head of the District Planning Committee of the Interior Ministry. Levy, who had been educated in a church mission school in Jerusalem and spoke fluent Arabic, was on excellent terms with the heads of the Eastern churches and was invariably present at church ceremonies – though this was not part of his formal duties. In the eyes of the churches he was a man of great power; it was Levy who issued the official documents which allowed the church dignitaries free passage – without security checks – back and forth across the Jordan River bridges, and Levy who headed the committee which vetted the building permits and plans recommended to him by the city.

With Levy, Kollek twice became involved in church affairs in an overtly political manner: in the election of the new Greek Patriarch in 1982 and, from that year onwards, in an increasingly complex

74

and unpleasant feud within the Armenian church.

In 1983, the old Greek Patriarch, Benedictos, who had enjoyed excellent relations with the Israelis, died. The most obvious contender for the office was his close follower, Vassilios – but he was not a strong church personality. Germanos, his chief rival, was said to be unfriendly to Israel. Initially, Raphael Levy supported Vassilios, but later – with the assistance of the Patriarch's secretary, Constantine, soon promoted Archbishop of Jordan – a third candidate emerged. This was Diodorus, who subsequently became Levy's protégé and the Greek Orthodox Patriarch of Jerusalem. The Jewish public took very little interest in the arcane proceedings of the Greek Orthodox Synod, but attentive readers of the press were to conclude that Germanos was a Palestinian nationalist, Vassilios 'favoured by Kollek' and Diodorus well thought of in Jordan, and were initially puzzled when the last was elected. It was only four years later, in a quite different context, that the full story of the elections was to emerge. Diodorus was elected, and proved a firm friend to the Israeli administration; no attention was paid to those officials who criticized the fact that Israelis had been drawn into church affairs.

Far more embarrassing was the intervention by Kollek and Levy on behalf of the Armenian archbishop Shahe Ajamian during his feud with the Armenian patriarch, Yegishe Derderian. Ajamian was Grand Sacristan of the Armenian community, a position which meant that he was in charge of all financial affairs between the Armenian Brotherhood and the municipal authorities. It was Ajamian who had handled the sale of church lands on the western slope outside the Old City walls, whose elegant landscaping is now universally admired by visitors to the city. Ajamian and the Patriarch sat in the front row at the opening of the exhibition at the Israeli Museum in 1969, when the ecclesiastical art and treasures of the small but wealthy community of the Armenian Quarter was put on show, and Ajamian spoke frequently at Israeli sponsored conferences on genocide and on the similarity of the fates of Jews and Armenians over the last century. Immensely rich, a collector of antiquities, charming and multilingual, he was an expansive host to Kollek's important foreign guests.

There was, however, an uglier side to the Armenian élite, which did not emerge until 1981. In that year, the Patriarch and Ajamian

fell out, and the Brotherhood decided to depose Ajamian for unspecified offences. Arab newspapers that attempted to describe what precisely he had done were sued by Ajamian, who also strongly objected
to their description of him as a collaborator with Israel.

Towards the end of the following year, Derderian appointed a
new Sacristan, an Australian citizen named Kareki Kazanjian. According to informed sources, both the city and the Interior Ministry
stepped up the pressure on the Patriarch; in an attempt to force
him to reinstate Ajamian, repair projects were held up, visas and
tax exemptions were withheld. The refusal to renew Kazanjian's visa,
and the fact that he was threatened with deportation, got into the
papers, as did the fact that Kollek, in June 1982, had recommended
the Interior Minister, Dr Burg, not to extend Kazanjian's stay in
the country. Faced with overt Israeli intervention in church affairs,
even the Greek Patriarch had to close ranks with the Latin and Armenian Patriarchs; they appealed to the President of Israel, Yitzhak
Navon, for an explanation. Finally, in February 1983, the Interior
Minister called a news conference to announce that he had ordered
the police *not* to deport Kazanjian, who subsequently remained in
Israel as Grand Sacristan, but without a visa, and as *persona non
grata* with the municipality. Ajamian continued to appear at Israeli
receptions and to use all his former privileges, including the limousine
allotted to him by the Brotherhood and the passage into Jordan free
of customs checks conferred on him by the Israelis.

In the Armenian Quarter — the only district of the Old City still
closed off behind its great gates at night — the feud between the supporters of the Patriarch and those of the Archbishop continued. In
May 1985, arsonists set fire to Ajamian's house; two years later,
a supporter of Ajamian's was stabbed to death. Since the Ajamian
affair relations between Israel and the Armenian church have soured,
while Kollek maintains that there is no one else of Ajamian's stature
to represent the community.

Meanwhile, however, the Mayor's supporters continued to claim
that Ajamian was a good friend of Israel, having voted against anti-
Israel resolutions at the World Council of Churches; and the intimacy
with the Greek Orthodox church was to prove useful for both sides.
Despite protests by Jerusalem conservationists, the Greek Orthodox
Patriarchate's plans for an ambitious extension to their head-

quarters were approved both at city and district levels, and the Greeks, for their part, continued to consult the Israelis every time it looked as though a church protest against Israeli policy was imminent. Any effective appeal to the President, or the outside world, by the churches of Jerusalem has to be signed by all the major figures of the Latin, Greek and Armenian churches, and for years the Greeks and Armenians tended to block anti-Israel protests. Despite the problems with the Armenians, the Greeks, who are more powerful, remain apprehensive of a possible rapprochement between Israel and the Catholics, and continue to be conciliatory.

One of the problems for Israel is the fear that the Christian churches and the Moslem clergy might one day join forces in protest against occurrences in the city under Israeli rule. This has happened only once; the Greek Orthodox blocked the crisis.

Kollek continues to defend his own right to intervene in church affairs 'if they endanger neighbourly relations' and to blast his critics: 'I can't stand that antiseptic mentality; I find it absolutely detestable. I feel free to act in any way that is in Israel's interest. The Jordanians did so far more than we do, they expelled a Patriarch. It's part of the tradition of the city.'

What is 'the tradition of the city' which Kollek sometimes invokes and sometimes wants to change? Jerusalem is historically a city of religious intrigue and bloodshed, a city of priests and peasants, only more recently of scholars and merchants as well. The Temple Mount, its contested jewel, is set in the very centre of a cradle of hills. The surrounding countryside, and even the desert, extend long fingers into the city from the east and south. Here, tens of little villages cling to their chosen place on the watershed. Jerusalem is a city where to stand on any one of the hilltops is to hear distant sounds – cock-crow, church bells, muezzins' calls, a motor-cycle backfiring, childrens' voices – from somewhere miles away across a valley. It is a city where the light is so crystalline that it almost eliminates perspective and the natural sense of distance, so that on certain days the Dead Sea, fifteen miles off but over three thousand feet down in the Jordan valley, seems within an hour's walk. Some of these perceptions, say those who care for them, could eventually be blocked by builders. Yet despite the environmentalists' complaints, the construction of the new suburbs – in principle an expansion and remodelling like that of every conqueror of Jerusalem – has not yet altered the landscape to the south and east. What it has done, however, is to invest all Israel's resources in the actual construction of the city and left little for the people.

Kollek envisaged as the dominant element in the population of his world city young, educated people who would find work and recreation within the capital. Today, despite the Mayor's efforts, there is a steady drain away from the capital to Tel Aviv, and even further afield, as well as to the Jewish satellite towns in the West Bank, whose establishment he firmly opposed from the outset. The Jewish population growth peaked in 1979. Since that year, more people have left Jerusalem than have arrived, and surveys indicate that they are precisely those young, qualified people Kollek wants to attract. The chief reasons are economic – lack of suitable employment, and the high cost of housing. Less than 10 per cent of the city's labour force are skilled industrial workers (less than half the average rate elsewhere in the country) and nearly half work in services, a far higher proportion than the national average. Jerusalem lives essentially on tourism, and as a centre of learning and bureaucracy.

But even where the cultural facilities are concerned, appearances are deceptive. Jerusalem has theatres and concert halls, but its radio orchestra has to struggle to compete with the Israel Philharmonic, domiciled in Tel Aviv, as does the small local theatre group, the Khan, with the larger theatre companies in Tel Aviv and Haifa. Artists prefer the laxer, warmer, more permissive atmosphere of Tel Aviv, and so do many young people who flee the oppressive silence of the pious Jerusalem Sabbath for the coast. Only the Israel Museum (open on Saturday mornings, despite everything) is a cultural institution with roots in Jerusalem, a place where every part of the population can find something of interest: art and archaeology for the secular, Judaica for the orthodox, oriental art and ethnography for Jews and Arabs whose cultural roots are in the East.

The two fastest growing groups in Jerusalem today are the ultra-orthodox (28 per cent of the Jewish population) and the Arabs (30 per cent of the total). City planners and sociologists mutter darkly of a 'non-Zionist' majority in the city. The ultra-orthodox contribute their piety, their tradition of scholarship, and a fierce desire to expel every trace of secularism from the city. The Arabs have contributed their labour. The new Jerusalem has been built by Arab labourers, stonemasons, carpenters and metal workers, very often working under Arab foremen and sub-contractors. To look at these two important communities is to see how little the pious, semi-rural Jerusalem has changed, but also how the effect of living in a semi-Western city has affected the relations of both groups with the secular, Jewish majority.

4

The View from the Seminary

TWICE A WEEK a little party of ultra-orthodox Jews – black-clothed, dark hats sheathed in plastic covers in rainy weather, long earlocks, prayer shawls under jackets – sets out from the offices of the Religious Council to tour the boundaries of Jerusalem. Not the boundaries as they are understood by map makers or urban planners, but the 110 kilometres which outline the areas where only Jews live. They take with them, in the back of their official pick-up trucks, ladders and bags of tools. Their job is to check on a wire strung between rusty poles on the outskirts of each Jewish district: poles between which, on the wire, at irregular intervals, little rags flutter.

This is the *eruv*, the Jewish perimeter, within which orthodox Jews are allowed to walk on the Sabbath while carrying their prayer books, gifts for friends, or other baggage needed on the journey. The peripheral suburbs have their own separate *eruv* if they are cut off from other Jews by Arab districts. The rags are necessary because the thin wire is often invisible against the background of further building, or hills; and sometimes, from a distance, the rags appear to be suspended in mid air, or flap wildly in the wind like birds' wings. In the winter, the *eruv* squad often has to repair equipment blown down by the fierce Jerusalem gales. Sometimes they find the entire length, poles and all, has gone. Arab villages, having seen the Jews approach with what looks like surveying equipment, suspect fresh expropriations and tear the *eruv* out.

Another orthodox work party sets out at four o'clock every morning to bring the produce of the surrounding Arab farming villages into the orthodox vegetable market in the Mea Shearim district. No other fruit or vegetable produce was edible by the *haredim* or ultra-orthodox before September 1987. For 1986/7 (the Jewish year runs from autumn to autumn) was according to the Jewish calendar a sabbatical year during which, according to the ordinance of *Shmitta*, the land must lie fallow. The economic implications of this have been worked out by rabbinical scholars who explain to the orthodox public how they can observe the ancient commandment under modern conditions.

All this meant little or nothing to the secular Jews of Jerusalem. What many did not even know is that, according to a rabbinical ruling accepted by the state, all the agricultural land in Israel is formally 'sold' in a fictitious procedure to non-Jewish landlords during the sabbatical year, so that its produce can be eaten by all observant Jews. The same procedure enables the cultivation of parks and gardens which – despite many adjustments permitted by religious law – would be reduced to wasteland were the commandment fully observed. Officially there is no planting of trees; in fact it continues in plastic bags filled with earth.

But this arrangement does not satisfy the *haredim*, the 'God-fearing' ultra-orthodox. The *haredim* buy their fruit and vegetables only after it is certified grown by bona fide gentiles. When a favourite vegetable is in short supply, the *haredim* import it. This year four hundred tons of carrots, eaten in a sugary dish called *tsimmes*, were imported from Holland.

All this made the year's work of the Urban Improvement Department much more complicated. Though almost all the city's gardeners are Arabs, they have been harassed when working in gardens in orthodox districts. *Shmitta* covers even the disposal of garbage; peelings must be left to dry out on open surfaces, and rigid separation must be made between the fresh and rotting remains of vegetables. Cleaning up the orthodox dustbins is that much more difficult.

Jerusalem of the *haredim* is not the city of parks and theatres, cafés and restaurants, libraries, swimming-pools and football grounds. For these amenities they have no use whatever. Their life is as hemmed in by the rituals of orthodoxy unchanged since medieval times, as the Sabbath walk is by the *eruv*. They take in no newspapers save their own orthodox publications; their bookshops sell nothing but talmudic works and commentaries on commentaries. Televisions are banned in *haredi* households. Their lives centre on the synagogue, the *yeshiva* or talmudic seminary, and the *mikve* or ritual bath.

In Mea Shearim, the archetypal orthodox district only a five-minute walk from City Hall, men's clothing shops sell the costumes worn by Jews for centuries in Eastern Europe: Polish fur-brimmed hats, black silk caftans, clothes guaranteed made with a particular mixture of flax and wool. Hairdressers in private houses shave the heads of married women and dress their wigs, dressmakers sew the clothes which cover them from neck to calves. Hardware shops sell decorations for scrolls of the Law, candelabra, amulets for protection against jealousy and the evil eye, or for 'health, prosperity and virility'. Collection boxes for charity are set in the walls; a man shaking a box at a street corner calls out 'Charity, charity brings redemption nearer.' Broadsheets in Hebrew and Yiddish are pasted on the walls of the narrow, winding main street.

One or two of the signs, put up at the entrances to the district, are in English, warning female tourists to dress modestly. Others, in Hebrew, forbid young secular couples to stroll the streets together. The local broadsheets inform the *haredim* of rabbinical decrees and edicts. One forbids trips to the sea as 'an offence against modesty'. 'The Day of Judgement approaches, and sins increase rather than virtues.' An elaborate *herem*, or anathema, running to forty lines and signed by members of the Salant and Bordaki rabbinical families, who have lived in Jerusalem for a hundred and eighty years, warns against sending children to schools where 'foreign languages and manners are taught'.

In the inner courtyards, and in the market, are other broadsheets put up by members of the Neturei Karta, the most fanatical of *haredi* groups, and the Eda Haredit, the 'Community of the God-fearing', who do not recognize the State of Israel, or those impious Zionists who anticipated the will of God by founding a state in the Holy Land 'before the coming of the Messiah'. Their message is more threatening: 'To join the army is according to our law a Jewish offence'; 'Jew, remember: whoever participates in the elections to the Zionist municipality participates in the destruction of the Temple.' 'This shop is closed [on Independence Day] in protest against thirty-seven years of the hoisting of the flag of rebellion against our Torah and that in the name of Israel, by the Nazionist blasphemers'; and, in a dark alley, scrawled on a wall, half-erased: 'Kollek – Nazi'.

Kollek, throughout his career as mayor, has been torn between a somewhat sentimental patronage of the *haredim* and a furious resentment of the trouble they have caused him. For the last fifteen years, says Kollek, he could have had a majority without the orthodox; but he maintains that, if possible, the ultra orthodox should be on

The reception at the Citadel: Kollek greets Yegishe Derderian, Armenian Patriarch. In the background, Raphael Levy, District Commissioner of the Ministry of the Interior.

Kollek with Cardinal John O'Connor of New York, spring 1987, in the entrance hall of the municipality. The mural behind him is the outer wall of the Council Chamber.

Members of the Jerusalem Committee survey new building from a hilltop on their fourth visit to Jerusalem, April 1978.

Kollek with Gerald Ford, former American president, in the Old City bazaar.

Kollek with flowers donated to a central park area by the people of Holland. The windmill in the background was put up by the nineteenth-century Jewish philanthropist, Sir Moses Montefiore.

Jews and Arabs in the Old City market.

The Western (Wailing) Wall. As the wall of the Temple Mount, this site is most sacred to Jews. It is also the wall of the Moslem Noble Sanctuary. In this picture, the minaret of one of the mosques is also visible.

The outer citadel: a new suburb in Jerusalem under construction; Arab flocks of goats in the foreground.

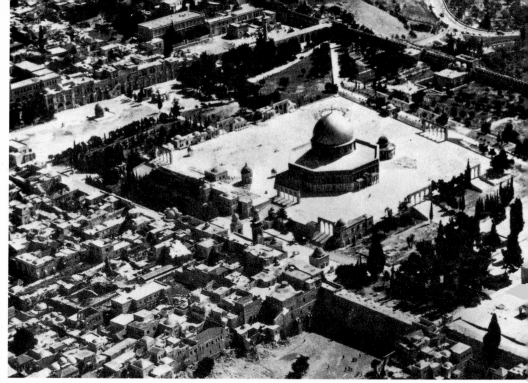

Aerial view of the Temple Mount, from the south-west. The Dome of the Rock is in the centre; the Al Aqsa mosque is on the right (*out of sight*); the Western Wall is in shadow in the foreground.

Inauguration of the Liberty Bell Garden, one of the largest projects of the Jerusalem Foundation, in 1978. In the background, under construction, the Jerusalem Sheraton Hotel.

Rejoicing of the Law: observant soldiers on leave celebrate in the streets as the Torah scrolls are borne aloft.

Orthodox demonstrators protest against Kollek's plans for a football stadium in Jerusalem. One placard reads: Stadium/idolatry/incest/bloodshed.

Kollek poses for an election picture tied up with rope to symbolize the limits to his powers imposed by the government.

The Admor of Gur, one of Kollek's most formidable opponents in the orthodox community.

Kollek with Anwar Nusseibeh, Palestinian leader of an old Jerusalem Arab family, at Nusseibeh's home.

The Old City: Arabs protest against Jewish rule in Jerusalem.

After a knifing in an Old City alley, Eliahu Amedi lies dying, 13 November 1986.

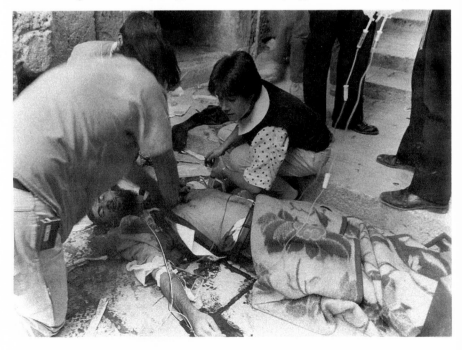

the City Council as a matter of principle. He has said that he sees the *haredim* as 'our grandfathers', a living reminder of the old Jewish communities in the Diaspora of past centuries. He has also said, on occasion, that the Mea Shearim people should 'have their bones broken' for making the work of the municipality and the police so impossible. He says that they deserve municipal services like any other group in the city, but, as a Zionist, he has always bitterly resented the fact that the Agudat Israel religious party kept its schools open on Independence Day and refuses to fly the national flag.

Whatever the ambivalence, he has acted like the old-style Labour politicians in courting orthodox support in his city coalitions. At one time it was the Agudat Israel, at another it was the Sephardi Torah Guardians whom Kollek mistakenly believed – on analogy with the old Sephardi community in Jerusalem – to be more tolerant than their Ashkenazi equivalents. He has had to accept a situation in which the religious orthodox in Israel have enormous power politically and institutionally. Although Israel has no constitution and there is no formal status for the Rabbinate as head of a state religion, this body, which has both Ashkenazi (Western) and Sephardi (Oriental) Chief Rabbis, is officially the religious leadership of the country. Rabbinical courts are the sole authority in the personal affairs of all Jewish Israelis – marriage, divorce, burial, etc. According to a political agreement between Ben Gurion and the religious parties immediately after the foundation of the state (the so-called status quo), there is no public transport on the Sabbath (save in Haifa, where a strongly left-wing leadership held out) and all cinemas, shops and restaurants are closed (though in Tel Aviv some have recently opened). But the ultra-orthodox, who recognize no authority but that of Jewish law, have tried to impose their will on the residents of Jerusalem in many other ways.

Kollek, who comes from a Jewish Central European family with the respectful but selective attitude to rabbinical tradition common to most Jews in the Diaspora since the Enlightenment, has learned bits and pieces of their philosophy over the years. 'They think that not observing the Sabbath hinders the coming of the Messiah,' he explained to an interviewer in 1985. His ideas of pluralism mean letting them alone to live their own lives, like the secular Jews and the Arabs. But for the *haredim*, the secular city is not only a temptation to be shunned, it is an offence against their very existence; for they see themselves as the unrecognized spiritual leaders of all Jews, responsible for the moral welfare of every Jew in the city – including that of Kollek himself. Closing a road off so that hedonist unbelievers will not drive through the districts of pious Jews on the Sabbath is not more than one small concession, in their view, to the righteousness of their cause. Like any other defenders of an absolute ideology, they will compromise on tactics but not on matters of substance, and almost every issue, in Jerusalem, is substantial: not only a synagogue to be built, or the sanctity of the Western Wall ensured, but the character of the whole city.

None of the *haredim* serves in the army; it has been calculated that the number of young men who claim exemption from military service as talmudic students (a claim recognized by Israel) exceeds the number of soldiers who fought in the battle for Jerusalem. Only a very small number of orthodox Jews serve in special units, where part of their time is devoted to talmudic study. (Orthodox here does not mean observant Jews; the observant Jews of Israel, distinguished externally by the wearing of skullcaps, perform army service like anyone else.) Save for the Neturei Karta and the Eda Haredit, most of the orthodox compromise with reality to the extent of voting both in national elections and for the religious factions in the municipality. Through the religious political parties, taxpayers' funds are channelled their way for the building of their institutions, the financing of their private educational system. Wealthy orthodox benefactors in the United States and elsewhere have contributed millions to the new, fortress-like seminaries which line the main roads of north Jerusalem where most of the orthodox Jews are settled.

Two broadsheets signed by the more fanatical rabbis indicate the most active form of rebellion against the Zionist state: one displays a photograph of police chasing *haredi* demonstrators near the Old City walls: 'Remember what Zionist Amalek did to you!' Another, more cautious, warns against throwing stones and burning down shops – a now increasing form of action against those who do not observe Jewish law. It is to prevent conflict and to enable orthodox Jews to enjoy their day of rest that on Sabbaths and festivals Mea Shearim, and several other religious districts, are closed off to motorists by police barriers.

Before 1967, ultra-orthodox Jews formed a self-centred minority in the city. There was little open confrontation, save just before election time. When the first mixed swimming-pool was opened in Jerusalem, far distant from the orthodox districts, there were protests; when the Israel Museum was opened in 1965, the orthodox rabbis protested that the sculpture garden was a display of 'graven images' and threatened to deface or remove the exhibits. But the swimming-pool remained open, the sculpture garden went untouched, and the secular community gradually came to think that the threats were mere rhetoric.

All this changed after 1967, when the orthodox community began growing more rapidly than any other sector of the Jewish community. After 1977, with their political alliance with the right-wing parties in the Knesset, they began to realize their strength. For the Mayor, the *haredim* became more and more of an encumbrance, an obstacle to his creation of a 'world city'. They did not want the archaeological sites 'restored': the diggers might violate Jewish graves. They did not welcome the big international hotels, and stepped up rabbinical inspection of their possibly unkosher kitchens. They objected to hotel celebrations on New Year's Eve, or – as it is called in Israel – Saint Sylvester, in the name of an ironically anti-Semitic pope. They objected to recreation centres and parks where young people of both sexes could mingle licentiously. They didn't want pluralism; they wanted piety, and penitence.

Kollek can deal with the Rabbis Porush, father and son, as one politician to another; not even the fact that the Mayor was snapped eating a hearty meal with a group of journalists on the eve of the 9th of Av – anniversary of the destruction of the Temple and a notable fast day – broke up the coalition between them. But when he ventured into the heart of rabbinical territory, things went less well.

A few years ago Kollek was having trouble with the orthodox community about a swimming-pool he wanted to put up in one of the outlying suburbs. He decided to visit one of the Hassidic dynastic leaders of the *haredi* community, the Admor of Gur. He was accompanied by an Israeli journalist, Tom Segev, who was at the time one of Kollek's aides. As Segev tells it, Kollek, hoping for co-operation from the Admor, launched into a recital of what he had done for the orthodox community in the city: he told the rabbi, as they sat in his book-lined study, how many synagogues he had built; how many *mikves*, how many *yeshivot* had enjoyed his help. The eminent rabbi sat silent, humming a little Hassidic tune to himself under his breath.

When Kollek had finished, the Admor pointed to a bowl of fruit on the table between them. 'Would you like a banana?' he enquired.

Kollek, irritated, shook his head, and continued: 'We closed off the roads for you in Mea Shearim...' 'Or would you like an *anona*? It's a new kind of fruit.' Kollek was bewildered. He continued for a while with the recital of his beneficence to the *haredim*. The Admor continued to hum beneath his breath, until finally, he took from his pocket an electronically powered gold watch and presented it to the Mayor. 'It's Japanese,' he explained politely.

Kollek had calculated forty minutes for his interview with the Admor and sent away his driver. He and Segev were out in the street after ten. 'My God,' he told his aide, 'he thinks I'm a *paritz* [lord of the manor in Eastern Europe]!'

The Mayor had met his match.

When Kollek became mayor in 1965, he showed himself far more prepared to conciliate the *haredim* than his predecessor. He agreed to close a number of roads leading to orthodox districts, and even near synagogues in other parts of town. Later he allotted part of the municipal budget to provide free milk for Torah classes of *haredi* children and premises for orthodox schools – though these are private and do not come under municipal control. Even then, there were secular Jews who objected to the concessions on principle, but Kollek overrode them. The *haredim* were part and parcel of the city, he said, and their feelings had to be considered; they were also taxpayers and deserved equal services.

The real troubles began after 1967, with the return of the Jews to the Western Wall. The *haredim* did not see the place as a historic monument, as did Israel's archaeologists, or even as a place of private prayer (which it had been according to tradition); they certainly did not see it as a place where Yehudi Menuhin could play a Bach partita or Ted Kennedy could insert a written prayer between the cracks of the great stones. They saw it as an orthodox synagogue over which they expected to exert exclusive rights. The *haredim* contested the archaeologists' right to dig anywhere around the wall, including its southern aspect; they needed no archaeological evidence for their beliefs. Eventually a compromise was reached by which the archaeologists' territory was limited to the south-west part of the Temple Mount's external walls. The Ministry of Religious Affairs took over the control of the Western Wall, including its northern extension, at the point where it is directly beneath buildings in the Moslem Quarter and others belonging to the Moslem authorities on the Mount. As this was sheltered, it could be used even during harsh winter weather – though not by women, since it formed a continuation of the men's section of the Wall.

The friction between the orthodox and the archaeologists was serious enough, but at least it was friction between Jews. The prospect of trouble with the Moslems was far graver. From the outset, the Moslem Wakf had been apprehensive of Israeli intentions regarding the Temple Mount. Though officially the Wakf did not recognize Israeli rule, talks were held between the Israeli authorities and the Wakf about all the archaeological and restoration work carried on in the vicinity of the Mount. In these talks, Kollek played a central part. An understanding was reached under which the Wakf would make no objection to Israeli work there, provided that its administrative position on the Temple Mount itself was absolute. This agreement, of great importance to Israel in the international sense, was endangered both by the amateur 'excavation' work of the Ministry of Religious Affairs and by the former chief army chaplain, later Ashkenazi Chief Rabbi, Shlomo Goren, who was among the first Jews to stage prayers on the Temple Mount.

The Wakf and the Supreme Moslem Council (a quasi-political body which had existed during the mandate and was renewed after 1967) were disturbed by the prospect that the excavation work undertaken might undermine the foundations of structures on the Mount itself. When they sent complaints and appeals to the Prime Minister, they were invited to tour the excavations and were reassured that skilled engineers were checking every stage of the work in that area to the south-west which lay directly beneath the Al Aqsa mosque. The situation was different on the north-west stretch, where the Ministry of Religious Affairs was in charge. Here, over the first few years after 1967, they continued to enlarge a corridor leading under a series of ancient Moslem buildings, among them the Makhama, the four-teenth-century courthouse building belonging to the Wakf. The Wakf not only regarded this as trespassing, but was indignant that a synagogue was being set up in what was virtually the cellar of a Wakf property. As the work proceeded, cracks began to appear in the upper floors of the Wakf buildings above, and only after a joint archaeological and municipal team was sent in to inspect the work were the amateur efforts of the orthodox archaeologists halted.

The question of whether Jews should pray on the Temple Mount is perhaps the single most inflammatory issue in the city. Moslems consider the area an Islamic sanctuary where the Israelis are guests; Jewish prayer suggests to them the first move towards an Israeli take-over of the site. Israel regards the Mount as in sovereign Israeli territory. The tacit understanding that Jews do not pray there rests on the very slender foundation of rabbinical opinion as to the probable site of the Holy of Holies. No Jew should ascend the Temple Mount (a notice put up by the Ministry of Religious Affairs announces) lest he tread accidentally on that place. Officially, the status quo (visits by Jews but no praying) evolved from an undertaking given by Levi Eshkol, Labour Prime Minister in the 1967 National Unity government, together with the Herut leader Menachem Begin, on the day after reunification. Apart from this, all that stops Jews from praying there is a police ruling, confirmed by the Supreme Court in 1970, that such behaviour is detrimental to public order.

But in Jewish practice no one rabbi is infallible, and there is no Jewish Pope. Rabbi Goren, after his own private researches, decided that he had located the exact site of the Holy of Holies and that prayer in other parts of the Mount was permissible. Goren was no obscure rabbinical student. As army chaplain in 1967, he had celebrated the Jewish return to the Western Wall by sounding blasts on a ram's horn (normally a ritual performed during the New Year service) and he had been a very articulate chief rabbi. The Moslem leadership assumed that if Rabbi Goren ascended the Mount and prayed there, he had government backing. There was no alternative but to send in the police and remove him.

But a very dangerous precedent had been set. Several small groups of worshippers, whose political intentions were more important than their orthodoxy, followed suit. They too were removed by the police.

At the beginning of 1976, a local magistrate, Ruth Or, heard an appeal by one of these groups and decided that – on strictly legal grounds – there was no reason to ban Jewish prayer on the Mount. When her decision was published, crowds of protesting Moslems gathered on the great square between the mosques, shouting slogans and threatening to attack any Jew who entered the precinct. Kollek immediately appealed to the government to call for a revision of the ruling, but it did nothing. Shopkeepers in the Old City went on strike, the metal shutters rolled down all over the bazaars and the pedlars disappeared from the streets. Schools in east Jerusalem closed in protest. Gangs of youths roamed the streets and threw stones at border police units called in to restore order. There were hundreds of arrests. West Bank municipal councils submitted their resignations. Abroad, Islamic nations protested, and the Secretary-General of the United Nations pledged himself to investigate the incident. All this because of an ill-considered decision by a minor member of the local judiciary, and the fact that the government decided that to voice any opinion would be to interfere in the judicial process or, worse still, to call in question Israel's sovereign rights over the Temple Mount. The Supreme Court saved the situation. It overruled Mrs Or's decision and restored the status quo. Since that time, the police have moved quickly to prevent any Jew opening a prayer book once past the Moors' Gate.

Among these activists are a more vocal group, many of them American orthodox Jews who joined the established orthodox community after 1967. They were also the main immigrant community of the post-1967 years. By 1977 a new sticker had appeared in the back windows of these immigrants' tax-free station-wagons which reads, 'We want Messiah Now.' It was not a joke.

Yom Kippur, the Day of Atonement, brings only a few hundred Jews to hold day-long services at the Western Wall. Most of those who observe the fast prefer the little neighbourhood synagogues where the majority of the city's Jews pray. The streets of west Jerusalem are empty and eerily silent. No secular Jew would provoke an observant neighbour by turning on the radio to a foreign station – Israel radio goes off the air – and the only Jews on wheels are the children on roller skates and skateboards who circle in the centre of the deserted main roads. Police barriers cut the roads linking Jewish and Arab districts. Outside the Dung Gate, the nearest entrance to the Wall precinct, Arab schoolboys play football, and the kiosks at the entrance to Silwan are open for the little groups of tourists; but the cart with sesame rolls, which normally stands at the Gate, is absent.

Painters used to represent the Wall as a towering cliff with worshippers clinging to its base. Kollek's clearance of the huge open space between the rest of the Old City and the Mount has dissipated that effect, and the wall is now just one side of an immense enclosure, bigger than Piazza San Marco in Venice, or one football field. The Wall plaza, as an extension of the Jewish Quarter, should be under the renovating hand of the company which develops that district. But in practice the Ministry of Religious Affairs and the Rabbinate, which regulates prayer at the Wall, have blocked every effort to landscape the space, introduce terracing (Safdie planned a terraced landscape) or even plant trees for shade and shelter. Instead, the plaza has an improvised look. A small fibreglass partition bisects the area nearest the wall, which is somewhat lower than the rest of the plaza, and separates the men's from the women's section. Trestle tables are brought out periodically into the men's section, where they serve the various groups who bring their own Torah scrolls. Women, who do not constitute a prayer group on their own, pray singly. At the entrance to their area is a kiosk containing heaps of scarves for any woman who arrives without the obligatory head covering.

Soldiers are deployed at all four entrances to the precinct; some sit with prayer books on their knees, glancing up as worshippers enter and checking bags. Across the square from the Wall is the nearest police station, where some of the worshippers, in prayer shawls, more comfortably seated, pray behind the barred windows. For hours, there are almost as many sightseers as worshippers. A handful of curious tourists gathers on the ramp leading up to the Moors Gate, the only entrance to the Mount controlled by Israel. The wooden doors to the Mount are closed and an alert detachment of police keeps an eye on a dozen worshippers who press close to the entrance: they are political militants, not the ultra orthodox. Conspicuous among them is Gershon Salomon, ex-member of the municipal council, who has made several provocative attempts to lead Jewish prayers beyond the gate in the past.

The worshippers below grow more numerous as the day wears on. Each group prays according to a different rhythm and a different music, according to its origins. Unlike the worship in a formal synagogue, where the rabbi and cantor lead the congregation, here it is each group, and, audibly, each man for himself. One strange figure, entirely alone, with no prayer book in his hand, revolves tirelessly at the centre of the crowds; he is a newly 'penitent' Jew improvising his own form of worship. It is only when dusk falls that each group sounds its *Shofar*, the ram's horn blast that ends the day's fasting and prayer, and the huge precinct begins to fill. Now hundreds of worshippers from the synagogues in the nearby Jewish Quarter move down the steps leading to the precinct, floodlights illuminate the ancient stones of the wall and, for the first time, the whole area comes alive.

The distance between Kollek's amiable view of Jewish tradition and the reality of ultra-orthodox practice is the distance between the Liberty Bell Garden, in the Cultural Mile, and Sabbath Square, in Mea Shearim, on the night of the Rejoicing of the Law.

The Rejoicing of the Law marks the end of the cyclical reading, in synagogues, of the first five books of the Bible – the Pentateuch. The celebration includes processions of men carrying the Scrolls of the Law around the reading desks in the synagogues, and, for the Hassidic Jews in particular, is accompanied by energetic dancing in the streets to music played on fiddles and recorders. In Israel, where all the festivals celebrated in the Diaspora take place in their natural environment – prayers for rain in northern Europe are absurd – the dancing spreads to the streets and even to organized festivities like that in the Liberty Bell Garden.

This garden, one of the principal recreation grounds of the city, lies on the site of the old Omariya olive grove (the trees were planted by the Greek Orthodox who own the land) just across the valley west of the Old City walls. There are lawns and little patios, stone walks covered by pergolas, a skating rink, an open air chessboard, a bandstand, a puppet theatre in a renovated railway carriage, a little walk dedicated to Martin Luther King and a mini-observatory dedicated to Billy Graham. At the centre of the Garden is a replica of the Philadelphia Liberty Bell, complete with the famous crack.

In a city where for reasons both of climate and temperament people tend to stay indoors or behind walls, Kollek has succeeded in drawing some fifteen thousand people every Saturday to the Liberty Bell Garden – donated by Americans. Like everything in Jerusalem the Garden has had its share of controversy: the plants trained over the pergolas grow only sparsely (some say there was sabotage at their planting); the Luther King olive trees were taken – unknown to the city officials – from land claimed by a West Bank village; and the Billy Graham observatory, with no written indications of its purpose, is almost completely shielded behind its circular wall. But the Garden is central enough, and varied enough in its attractions, to bring Jews and Arabs of all ages together at weekends.

On the night of the Rejoicing of the Law, the Garden overflows with an eager audience for the dancing – many of them the city's mainstream observant Jews. A platform has been set up near the skating rink and serves as a bandstand and dance floor, and the space facing it is jammed with the standing spectators. Every public organization in the city has sent its representatives to the celebration organized by the Rabbinate, the Religious Council and the Torah Culture Department of the municipality to perform an overture to the main programme, the traditional *hakafot* or round dances performed by Jews from all the different communities in Jerusalem. Among them is the Mayor, left hand outstretched on the shoulder of the official in front of him, right arm grasping the heavy, red velvet clad Torah scrolls. Kollek has a look of grim determination on his face; the scrolls are heavy with the weight of Jewish history and hundreds of commandments, the eternal subject of debate and elaboration for talmudic scholars.

Meanwhile, in Mea Shearim, the scene is different. Sabbath Square, the central place of ultra-orthodox demonstrations, is not a square but a crossroads at the bottom of a steep hill. There is no garden here; since 1969 the *haredim* have made it clear that they disapprove of trees and bushes behind which young people might make assignations – and worse.

Sabbath Square is flanked by hardware shops, the Great Soup Kitchen of a famous Eastern European charity and a branch of the Discount Bank. Here, too, a bandstand has been erected on the slope overlooking the crossroads and the traffic lights which flash orange periodically over the deserted intersection – the police have cordoned off the area. Amplifiers relay the Hassidic melodies, with their lilting, gypsy rhythm, so inviting that an observer might expect the crowds milling about beneath the bandstand to leap into motion. But nothing happens.

At the front of the bandstand, near the fiddlers, a row of venerable rabbis, all in their festival gear, white beards flowing, have taken their seats. Occasionally they exchange a remark. But for most of the time they sit stiffly, staring straight in front of them, their eyes fixed on the possibly hypnotic flashing of the traffic lights. No one dances. The slope is divided by more police barriers, with signs and arrows directing MEN and WOMEN to opposite sides. The division appears to apply to the young people, for there are many families, the fathers pushing prams with at least two or three older toddlers clinging to the sides and the mothers carrying string bags with bottles of weak tea and packets of biscuits. When the band stops, Rabbi Meir Porush, star of the evening, comes forward. The young leader of the Agudat Israel opposition in the City Council makes a party political speech, describing the synagogues and classrooms put up thanks to Agudat Israel lobbying, and their battles with the 'forces of the Left' who threaten constantly to screen films on the Sabbath and build swimming-pools near orthodox homes.

The real Rejoicing of the Law is somewhere else, deep in the ill-lit courtyards behind the main streets. Women and children cluster in the dark outside the lighted windows of the little synagogues where the *yeshivah bochers*, the young talmudic students, chant and leap around the prayer desks, waving the scrolls above them as if they were as light as drum majors' batons.

To the south of the city, in the Baka'a district off the Bethlehem road, there is yet another form of celebration. In the new Reform congregation, most of whom are immigrants from the United States, women will not agree to be mere observers, faces pressed to the window panes. In Reform synagogues, there are no partitions separating men and women. Women sometimes officiate as cantors, or – abroad – even as rabbis, and they participate quite openly in the Rejoicing of the Law.

Reform Jews are as welcome in orthodox ruled Jerusalem as the early Christians were in Rome. Baka'a has no catacombs, but the

Reform have found temporary shelter in the basement of the local community centre. In the nearby orthodox synagogue, where the veteran Sephardi congregation gathers, the rabbi gets word of the terrible spectacle of 'uncovered' women with Torah scrolls in their arms dancing together with the men. A detachment sets out, the rabbi at their head; they enter the basement, join in the dancing, then try to wrest the scrolls from the arms of the indignant Reform members. There is a scuffle and the police are called. Next day, there is a truce: Kollek, always the referee, announces that he will help the Reform rabbi find more suitable quarters – in the same district. But no such drastic move is needed: the Reform rabbi's olive branch being, temporarily at least, accepted.

Kollek has strong ties to the American Jewish community, many of whom attend Reform synagogues, and he resents the orthodox opposition. Only a week or so after the Baka'a incident an extension is opened to the elegant Hebrew Union College (Reform) building which stands on more neutral ground, near the King David Hotel. Kollek, the guest of honour, is presented with another honorary doctorate to add to his collection. The American Ambassador, Thomas Pickering, reads a telegram from the administration congratulating the Reform movement in Israel on its growing presence.

In Mea Shearim, a new poster appears. Signed by the Sephardi Chief Rabbi, Mordechai Eliahu, it explains that members of the Reform movement are not Jews at all, but Gentiles. The Rabbi proclaims that the abuse of the Jewish religion by the Reform synagogue, its simplified conversion rituals and its marriage ceremonies endanger the very basis of Judaism, and allow many strangers in to the fold. 'The acceptance of these people leads, heaven forbid, to intermarriage, and Gentile children concealed among us who are falsely known as Jews.'

The growing population of the *haredim* in the city has not just affected the style of celebration of the Jewish holidays. It has fundamentally influenced – and often changed – the planning of the city.

As the city grew, orthodox districts which were once on the outskirts were in their turn enclosed and ringed with new roads – particularly those to the north of the city, on the bare, rocky hillsides to the east of the main road to Tel Aviv. This was probably the least attractive site for building before 1967; the orthodox chose it for its very remoteness. But in 1978 tractors appeared in the valley beneath the orthodox suburb of Kiryat Zanz, and began levelling the ground for a six-lane highway to Ramot, one of the new peripheral suburbs.

In designing this road the municipal planners had two objects. The obvious one was to link the centre of town with the new suburb; the second was to prevent the orthodox suburbs spreading into the valley area, designed as part of a green belt around Jerusalem.

There was already a road to the Ramot suburb. It passed equally close to another orthodox district, Sanhedria Murhevet, inhabited by Jewish immigrants from America and Russia. But Kiryat Zanz was inhabited by several of the most extreme of all the *haredim*, descended from those Eastern European rabbinical sects which have dominated Jerusalem orthodoxy since the nineteenth century. Their leaders now vied with one another to oppose the construction of the highway which, they declared, was an open provocation to their Sabbath observance.

No traveller on the Ramot road could take this argument at its face value. The road curved through a valley deep below the outermost blocks of orthodox flats. In order to be thoroughly provoked and disturbed, the tenants had to leave their own streets, climb down a steep hillside, and deliberately go out on to the road on the Sabbath.

Every Saturday, groups of black-clothed demonstrators put up barricades and threw stones at passing motorists. Crowds of young scholars gathered by the roadside to shout and wave their fists at drivers. Questions were asked in the Knesset and Kollek was harassed in the City Council. Meanwhile, the tenants of Sanhedria Murhevet were annoyed that traffic was now passing more frequently on *their* side of the valley. They also climbed down on to the road and held prayer services there on the Sabbath. Rabbis refused to rule as to which of the two neighbourhoods should give way. The stone throwing and shouting became a weekly performance, and the rabbis argued that if stones were thrown by boys under thirteen (by religious law not yet responsible for their actions) they should not be condemned, as the action 'was for a worthy purpose'.

Kollek refused to be intimidated. The orthodox obviously expected him to close off the road, as he had done many times before. But this was a major arterial road. At first he sent out the city gardeners to plant saplings by the roadside, hoping that trees would eventually hide the offending view from orthodox eyes. The saplings were uprooted. Thousands of new orthodox recruits from the older districts marched out to Kiryat Zanz on the Sabbath, straight from the synagogue to the front line. The shouts were audible from balconies of houses miles away. The riot police were called in. Ramot residents threatened to set dogs on the orthodox if they continued stoning the cars. The orthodox threatened to burn down Ramot.

Kollek called in professors from the Hebrew University and the Haifa Technion, Israel's major engineering faculty. Eventually a new bypass was built, costing the city a hundred thousand dollars. Orthodox honour was satisfied; the seminarists retreated uphill. The six-lane Ramot highway remained open. The new bypass was never used.

Kollek had won that battle, at some financial cost to the city. He was to lose a far grander one: the battle of the Jerusalem Stadium. Kollek was to term this 'the most serious crisis in thirteen years of office'.

Soccer is no less of a passion in Jerusalem than elsewhere in the world. In Israel it has an extra, political dimension, for all the teams are run and financed by political parties, so that sporting, local and political loyalties are involved.

Shortly after the Six Day War, the City Council voted to build a large modern football stadium to replace the existing facilities: two small, dilapidated grounds — one in a residential suburb, the other at the local YMCA in the centre of the western city. Near both these grounds cars jammed the pavements every Saturday afternoon, and the roars of triumph or disgust were audible for miles around.

The problem was where to put the new, 25,000-seat stadium. A number of vacant sites were reviewed: one was discovered to be church land, another to involve expropriation of Arab orchards; a third had been promised to the local bus company as garage space, and a fourth site was to become a commercial centre. Finally the ideal site was found, on government-owned land in north-east Jerusalem, accessible both from central Jerusalem and (for out of town spectators) from the road to Tel Aviv.

When the proposal was put to the public, there were at first only a few mild objections. There was already a perfectly good large stadium at the Hebrew University campus in the west; but the grounds were too visible from the surrounding hillsides and – for Kollek's own peace of mind – far too near the Museum's Sculpture Garden.

The secular objections were laid aside. But by this time the orthodox community was up in arms. The Agudat Israel argued that the noise would disturb the Sabbath peace of the orthodox districts about half a mile away. Kollek proposed that the games be played late in the evening, and the Agudat Israel was inclined to give way. Not so the ultimate authority among the *haredim*, the Council of Sages. The venerable rabbis were uninterested in political gains for the Agudat Israel, uninterested in the National Religious Party (the more moderate religious politicians in the Knesset) who controlled the Ministry of the Interior and hence regional planning. What concerned the rabbis was the principle of the thing. They proclaimed football a hedonist, Greek pleasure forbidden within the precincts of the Holy City. American orthodox rabbis, the big fund-raisers for the Jerusalem orthodox, echoed the Sages' warnings. The Agudat Israel toed the line. Together with the most extremist orthodox sect in the city, the Eda Haredit, they sponsored the largest demonstration ever held in Jerusalem. Fifty thousand *haredim* gathered in the streets around Sabbath Square, shouting, praying and brandishing slogans. 'Kollek: take your stadium to Mount Olympus, where Greek culture is welcome', read one banner. The little Jewish boys waving red flags, complete with hammer and sickle, to encourage the Labour Party's soccer teams playing at the YMCA grounds near the King David Hotel would have been surprised to learn that they represented Greek culture, but there was no redress.

Both Chief Rabbis of Israel called on Kollek to abandon the plan for the stadium because 'it would imbue Jerusalem with Hellenistic culture, the spirit which our forefathers fought throughout history'. Kollek consulted scholarly books and argued that there had been Jewish philosophers who had encouraged physical culture. Some of the little orthodox boys, in their heavy black clothes and long earlocks, who kick tin cans around surreptitiously in the alleys of Mea Shearim, might have agreed with him, but their elders did not. The Neturei Karta threatened to excommunicate Kollek from the Jewish community in the 'Rod of Fire' kabalist ceremony in which every curse 'from Moses to the present day' would be called down on his head by three rabbis, while black rams' horns were sounded and black candles burned. This curse had most recently been invoked, they said, against the heads of a Jerusalem burial society twenty years earlier; both had died within the week.

On a more prosaic level, the Agudat Israel leader Menachem Porush appealed to the then Prime Minister, Menachem Begin, the right-wing leader who was head of a coalition with the religious parties in the Knesset. What followed was perhaps the most flagrant political intervention in municipal affairs during Kollek's term of office. Begin sent Kollek a letter, in August 1979, at the height of the crisis; it said he would be grateful if 'in the cause of understanding between the various inhabitants of Jerusalem and the restoration of tranquillity in the capital' Kollek would stop work on the stadium for two months while alternative accommodation was found and 'all the financial aspects of the matter' were studied. This was a clear reference to the grant which had been promised to Kollek by the Minister of Education some time earlier as a matching sum for money promised to the Foundation – which together would have financed the stadium construction. If Kollek had not agreed, he says, 'I would have been left with a hole in the ground.'

The football clubs, and the fans, were surprisingly silent. There was no counter demonstration. They seem to have assumed, with everyone else, that Kollek was invincible.

This was not the end of the story. Kollek now tried, with Raphael Levy, the official in charge of the District Planning Committee, to push through the enlargement of the disused stadium in the southern residential district, Katamon. But here he had reckoned without the opposition of the local residents who had learned, by the end of the 1970s, that they were not just the passive objects of government or municipal decision. Finally Kollek found another site, at Manhat, on the extreme western border of the city; the nearest orthodox district was on a hilltop across a wide valley, separated from the site by a huge field of electricity pylons. But this too has been opposed by the orthodox. Worse still, the Ministry of the Interior has now passed from the control of the National Religious Party, the moderates led by the jovial, German-born Dr Burg, with whom Kollek had excellent relations, to the Sephardi Torah Guardians, who are far more extreme.

Today, the Jerusalem Labour team still plays on the YMCA field, while the right-wing Betar team, with its thirty thousand supporters, have to travel every Saturday – in flagrant defiance of Jewish law – to the Bloomfield Stadium in Jaffa.

'It was the defeat over the stadium which made Teddy decide not to form another coalition with the Agudat Israel,' says its veteran leader, Rabbi Menachem Porush. 'He was very angry. I admire him for all he has contributed to Jerusalem, his talent for public relations. But not as an administrator. He should have understood that Jerusalem isn't Monte Carlo, or Paris. The Likud, we feel, is more sympathetic to us today than Labour. The Labour people can't free themselves from their background – you know, the Russian Revolution, communism, anti-religious socialism.

'We have no interest in sports; our pleasure is in the *yeshiva*. There is a great revival of religion today in Israel, a flight from the secular. You won't find a talmudic student today reading poems by Bialik, or [Zionist philosophy] by Ahad HaAm. We're reprinting works of scholarship today that haven't been read for three hundred years. Secular nationalism has proved empty. They say that we orthodox are driving people away from Jerusalem; but they leave for other reasons, they leave the country too. It's only religion which keeps people here.'

Kollek's views on the religious revival are different. 'This is a period of fanaticism, a return to religious fundamentalism not only in Israel but abroad, in the Christian church and in Islam as well as in Judaism. It is more noticeable to us, as Zionists, as we built a democratic state in which we had high respect for the religious, but where all could live their own lives. There's no symmetry here – we tolerate the religious, but they don't tolerate us.'

Emboldened by their victory over the stadium, the *haredim* attempted to end the excavations beyond the southern wall of the Temple Mount, in the ancient City of David. They argued that the entire site covered Jewish graves and should remain untouched. The archaeologists defended academic freedom and research, and on this issue, connected as it was with the unveiling of Jewish historical sites in Jerusalem, the politicians did not take the side of the orthodox.

The mounted police (Amalek) chased away the demonstrators.

But violence in the orthodox camp grew steadily. Non-orthodox tenants living in orthodox districts were threatened, and four of their houses were vandalized and two burned down in 1982. During the winter of 1982/3, the driver of a car passing near a religious district – but not beyond the police barriers – was badly injured when a stone thrown through his windshield fractured his skull. And in October 1983, Kollek himself was the victim of an attack.

The background to the incident was a fresh argument about sports facilities in the city; but this was clearly a pretext for the hatred many *haredim* now felt for the Mayor. Kollek was literally ambushed. As he left a synagogue he had been visiting in the Bukharan Quarter, a gang of orthodox men tripped him and knocked him to the ground. He was kicked and spat on by a crowd; helped to his feet by an aide, he was knocked down for the second time. Kollek lodged a complaint with the police, but no arrests were made. The violence condoned by the ultra-orthodox rabbis as 'the law for the unbeliever' is tacitly supported by the *haredi* community as a whole, though the perpetrators are few. The police complain that it is impossible to infiltrate the ultra-orthodox communities, where every face is known and a wall of complicity protects the offenders.

Under pressures such as these, municipal policy on housing has changed. Secular and ultra-orthodox Jews, it is now agreed, cannot live together. Though in planning terms there is no such thing as a 'religious district', both municipal planners and the Housing Ministry now set aside specific areas for orthodox housing. These are planned away from main traffic arteries, and far from sports grounds and swimming-pools. Where private contractors are concerned, the contracts drawn up specify that the clients are expected to observe the Sabbath and to refrain from behaviour offensive to the orthodox – though such clauses cannot be enforced by law. In fact any non-orthodox family which accidentally finds itself in an orthodox district is soon 'persuaded' to move.

Kollek himself has become the target of criticism not only by the Agudat Israel who continue to maintain that they are discriminated against in the municipal budget, but by the secular, who see him as responsible for orthodox incursions into secular districts where, experience has shown, they rapidly take over entire roads and areas.

In the Mahane Yehuda wholesale market, young seminarists from a nearby orthodox district circulate on Friday afternoons and force the stall owners to close down before they have finished the day's sales, well in advance of the Sabbath. They have bought up whole buildings in other parts of town to serve as seminaries, bringing entire neighbourhoods to a standstill on the only day of the week when most Israelis want to drive out to see friends, sunbathe on their porches, or play their radios.

In French Hill, one of the first of the post-1967 suburbs, groups of residents have banded together against the city's decision to build a large new synagogue complex near the commercial centre, on the main road. An open letter to Kollek in winter 1986, signed by thirty-six leading residents including university professors and high-ranking army officers, called on the Mayor to rescind the permit and instead build a community centre for the secular majority. They wrote: 'We support the planning of a prayer centre for the orthodox residents of the district, but we object strongly to the attempt, by militant orthodox circles from outside the district, to dictate its way of life to the whole population. We will not agree to this happening on French Hill. In a short while it will be almost impossible to breathe freely in this city. We will not remain silent, for this is a vital issue.'

In April 1985 Kollek met with a group of angry Jewish residents who had formed a league against orthodox violence. He agreed to set up a fund to compensate the victims, to repair 'moderate damage' caused by the seminarists, and to reconsider the issue of road closure on Sabbaths. But when news of the meeting leaked out, the orthodox factions on the City Council raised an outcry. No closed roads were reopened.

By this time, the ultra-orthodox had another bone to pick with Kollek, and this time they were more widely supported. Kollek's generous welcome to the various Protestant groups who had arrived in the city in recent years revived fears of missionary activity. Many of the orthodox Jews in Jerusalem are descendants of those very families who fought the missions most stoutly in the second half of the nineteenth century. A special organization 'YadLe Achim' (A Hand to our Brothers) was set up to monitor any missionary work in the city, and – predictably – one of the first acts of the Begin government was to pass the Missionary Law in December 1977, which forbade any attempts to proselytize accompanied by 'financial inducements'. Israel is not exceptional in passing such laws, which exist throughout the Arab world and in Greece and Turkey. But there has been hardly any missionary work in Israel in recent years, and the law provoked protests in the World Council of Churches.

In the spring of 1985, Dr Burg, the Minister of the Interior, the then Foreign Minister Yitzhak Shamir and other government officials supported a proposal from the American Mormons to build an extension to the Brigham Young University of Salt Lake City on the slopes of Mount Scopus. Kollek also agreed to the proposal. The blueprint for the large complex, including dormitories and sports grounds, passed both the local and district planning committees which included representatives from the religious parties. It was only when the construction started that the orthodox sat up and took notice, and the outcry began. The prospect of an ostentatious Mormon presence in Jerusalem infuriated not only the Jewish orthodox but the veteran Christian communities of the city, to say nothing of the Palestinian militants who said that if the Jews wanted to be so generous to the Mormons, they could allot them ground in west Jerusalem and not that expropriated from the Moslems. The Apostolic Delegate registered a formal protest on 'environmental grounds' alone; privately, however, Christian churchmen spoke of the new campus as 'an outrage'. Said one, 'They are not Christians, and they have no traditional community in the city.' Even secular Jews were troubled by the fact that the Mormons, who baptize the living in the name of the dead, had asked the Israel Holocaust Authority, Yad Vashem, for lists of those who had died in the concentration camps (the request was turned down).

Kollek (who was only one of those backing the project) was the target for most criticism because he had stood up for the Mormons as a matter of principle, and he was in an awkward situation. The other officials tried to dissociate themselves from the project. The protests of the orthodox had provoked a counter protest in the name of religious liberty from 127 members of the American Congress. He and his supporters argued that the business was a storm in a teacup, and that Mormon students had been visiting Jerusalem for years without a single conversion. But in the overheated atmosphere of Jerusalem the incident produced yet one more odd alliance: this time between YadLe Achim in the audience as supporters, and members of the Christian churches, who appeared at a press conference in July 1985. In November, the *haredim* staged another of their huge demonstrations, and Kollek had to write to the Mormon leaders in Salt Lake City explaining the sensitivity of the issue, and insisting that they provide a written guarantee that no attempts would be made on the campus to convert the Jews of Jerusalem.

The orthodox threatened to stop any Jew setting foot on the Mormon campus, causing yet more tensions in a city which scarcely needed them. Orthodox violence increased almost daily. In late 1986, the young seminarists who took it on themselves to chastise the ungodly began, for the first time since 1965, to carry out hit and run operations outside their own districts. In 1965, before Kollek's first elections, they had stoned buses in the main streets of the city. This time the objects of their fury were the new bus shelters recently put up all over the city, which, with their plexiglass frames, protected the passengers from the icy gales that blow through Jerusalem in winter and from the blazing sun of summer.

The Tel Aviv firm which supplied the shelters had decorated the frames with fashion advertisements showing girls in bathing costumes, men and women in tight-fitting jeans, and other photographs the orthodox considered obscenely provocative.

The pious punishment squads circulated in get-away cars, with jerrycans of kerosene, rags and matches, and within a few weeks, forty of the new shelters were burned out, leaving Jerusalem travellers to squat on the twisted metal remains of the plastic benches and shiver in the driving rain coming through the ruined frames. Only a couple of seminarists caught in the act were punished; all were defended by the rabbis. At some cost to the city, the suppliers replaced the advertisements with photographs of mayonnaise and tomatoes, or, as one observer commented, obscene pictures of an undressed salad and a salad dressing.

This new battle was too ridiculous to merit attention, save by the soaked and shivering bus passengers. Another, very serious development in the ultra-orthodox community was now to affect the most sensitive area of Jewish-Arab relations in the city. This was the renewal of the old Jewish seminaries in the Moslem Quarter of the Old City.

Until violent clashes between Arabs and Jews drove them out during the 1930s, some fifteen hundred Jews had lived in the Moslem quarter of the Old City, where there were many Jewish foundations: seminaries, orphanages and hospitals. Moslem owners took over the Jewish properties and after 1948 they passed into the control of the Jordanian Custodian of Enemy Property, just as Arab houses in west Jerusalem were administered by his Israeli counterpart.

Despite its activities in the Jewish Quarter, the Israeli government made no move after 1967 to oust Arab tenants from what had originally been Jewish property in the Moslem Quarter. But in 1978 an orthodox organization called Ateret LeYoshna (The Crown of Old) began to buy out tenants of these houses in areas of the Moslem Quarter nearest to the Western Wall: both those which had previously belonged to Jewish owners, and other properties near them. The Israel Lands Authority and other government institutions, as well as orthodox institutions in Israel and abroad, provided the funds. Over the next decade some $800,000 was spent on the purchase of buildings, many of which were little better than hovels. As both Jordan and the PLO threaten punishment to any Arab who sells property to Jews, the deals were usually carried out through third parties. The new tenants were ultra-orthodox seminarists, who made no secret of the fact that they wanted to 're-establish a large Jewish presence' in the Moslem Quarter, and in the end to encircle the Wall from all sides. Moslems have a very similar feeling that they must remain in the Old City to 'protect the mosques' on the Temple Mount from the Jews.

At first there was no open conflict, though some local Arabs insisted that houses had been occupied by the seminarists when their owners were absent, or had died. But late in 1982, a new and sinister seminary appeared in the Moslem Quarter.

The seminary was first called The Blessing of Abraham and then Return O Sons, an acknowledgement of the fact that many of its members did not belong to the veteran orthodox community but were newly observant Jews, or 'penitents' — part of a new Israeli trend that developed during the 1970s in which thousands of young Jews 'returned' to an ultra-orthodox, and often fanatical, form of Judaism.

The Penitent Sons began, as they continued, by force. They settled first on the property of another reclaimed Jewish seminary (called Eternal Life) whose members tried to evict them first by legal means and then by force. Both manoeuvres failed, partly because the police are reluctant to intervene in orthodox squabbles, and partly because many of the Penitent Sons were former members of crack army units who, beneath their beards and prayer shawls were – for talmudic students – remarkably muscular.

Eventually Eternal Life gave in and signed a contract admitting the Penitent Sons as sub-tenants of a few rooms above a courtyard on their property. All around that courtyard, and beneath the rented rooms, were Arab families, whose lives were now to be exposed to daily provocation and harassment, designed to make them leave and turn over their property to the Sons.

Many of these Penitents were violent and uncontrollable men – ex-delinquents, who had chosen a particular sect to follow because of the mystical experience it promised. They claimed to be followers of Rabbi Nahman of Bratslav, a nineteenth-century Ukrainian Hassid, or Jewish mystic, who believed himself to be one of a messianic line. Rabbi Nahman had set faith above philosophy and thought, and advocated a direct dialogue with the Deity, as well as the observation of the rituals prescribed by Jewish law. Genuine descendants of the Bratslav sect deny that the group which entered the Moslem Quarter in 1982 had any real understanding of the tradition; but the Bratslav *hassidim* are different from all other orthodox groups in that they acknowledge no living rabbi or pastor. In Yiddish, for this reason, they are nicknamed 'the dead *hassidim*'; and the Penitent Sons lived up to the name, sowing destruction wherever they went.

Their notion of worship was to pray as loudly as possible, often standing on the rooftops until after midnight singing, shouting and banging on saucepan lids or on drums. They often went out into the open fields round Jerusalem, or into the desert, to shout prayers and appeals to their Maker. There was little peace for their neighbours, who complained repeatedly to the police that the Sons had broken their windows and thrown all kinds of filth, including their own excrement, into their houses. The Sons denied all charges and the police made no arrests. The Arab family which suffered most was the Abu Almiali clan whose property the Sons coveted in particular. They made repeated, but unsuccessful, attempts to persuade this family to sell out to them and move away. One night in September 1983 the elderly Fatma Abu Almiali was found lying in the main room of her house with a fractured skull and wounds all over her body from a sharp instrument. According to the family, as they were carrying her out of the house, the Sons pelted them with stones and bottles from the windows of the seminary.

While she lay in hospital, forty Arabs came in a delegation to Kollek and begged him to find a way of removing the Sons' seminary from the Arab quarter. They were prepared for any other religious group or family to move in, they said, but they were convinced that the Sons were mentally disturbed and dangerous. Kollek promised them police protection and said that he would meet with police officials and the two Chief Rabbis. He also took the opportunity to demand that they restrain other Arabs of the Old City who had been throwing stones at Jews passing through the alleys.

Kollek, with the backing of a majority of his City Council, requested that the seminary be removed from the Moslem Quarter. The police refused to evacuate the Sons. Kollek lobbied the Chief Rabbis, the Prime Minister, the Minister of the Interior and leading members of the Labour Party. All argued that it would be necessary to bring in the army to remove the Sons and that this was impossible. Kollek argued not only against this particular seminary, but against 'resettlement' of this kind in the Moslem Quarter. He told the Ministerial Committee on Jerusalem that the move was a dangerous precedent, as much property in Jewish Jerusalem also belonged to Arabs and that they might one day seek its return. But no one saw this as an urgent threat, and to remove Jews – any Jews – from an area which had been 'reclaimed' was politically inexpedient. The committee was prepared only to recommend that further purchases in the Moslem Quarter be made by families, and not by institutions, and that these purchases be made only in the immediate environment of the Jewish Quarter. But the new committee which was to supervise the implementations of these resolutions was not set up.

Meanwhile, Fatma Abu Almiali lay in hospital. The Israel Association for Civil Rights took an interest in the case. The seminarists had been questioned by the police, but had insisted that the woman had been hurt by stones thrown by Arab rioters. The Association pointed out that the woman had been stabbed, and enquired why the police were doing nothing further about the case. The police replied that they were unable to continue their investigation 'as the woman's memory was impaired'. After a month, she died. The police file was closed 'for lack of evidence'.

In his next election manifesto, Kollek included a clause stating that the faction opposed Jewish settlement in the Moslem Quarter, but he and his followers were alone in their concern. Late in 1986, as will be seen, Jerusalem was to pay a heavy price for the government's failure to crack down on a few young thugs out to terrorize their Arab neighbours.

5

The View from the East

IN THE EARLIEST HOURS of the morning, Jerusalem belongs to the Arabs. From east Jerusalem and villages between the municipal boundaries, and from the West Bank towns – Ramallah, Bethlehem, Hebron – come trucks and taxis, some with the blue number plates of the West Bank, taking thousands of Arab workers to the building sites, hotels and factories of Jewish Jerusalem. Most are from villages within the Jerusalem area; some seven hundred a day come in from outside the city. The great majority, those from Israeli Jerusalem, are regular employees, with union rights, national insurance and health-care cards. But a few tens of day labourers solicit for work at the 'slave market', a long stone wall which marks the old frontier near the former Mandelbaum Gate – now a mere crossroads. Here Jewish contractors come to pick up workers at rates up to 40 per cent less than standard pay; here too police jeeps stop frequently to check the Arabs' papers and sometimes to fine them for 'blocking a public thoroughfare'.

Each Friday morning, from four o'clock, hundreds of sheep, marked with red henna and branded, are herded on to a platform under the north-eastern edge of the Old City walls, opposite the Rockefeller Museum, at the heart of the eastern city. Some of the sheep find their way into Jewish restaurants and butchers' shops via one of the few shared facilities, the Jerusalem slaughterhouse, where Jews and Arabs work on alternate days. At Mount Scopus, the Hebrew University campus, Arab cleaning workers, whose regular job is as shepherds from the local villages, swab the corridors before the first students arrive. Trucks gather at the gates of the Old City with crates of fruit and vegetables for the great vaulted markets patronized chiefly by the Arabs; the Jews have their own wholesale market, Mahane Yehuda, at the western side of the city.

At six o'clock on a hot September morning, the streets are already stifling, but in the covered, vaulted markets of the Old City, the air is cool. In a stable off the vegetable market, two municipal workers whose salary is paid in barley are harnessed for work: they are the Old City donkeys, who are better fitted for hauling garbage through the alleys, with their hundreds of steps, than the latest hydraulic truck imported from Switzerland.

In a tiny office under a dome in one of the side streets near the Seventh Station of the Cross, the head of the Sanitation Department, Meir Anshmister, reviews the local cleaning squad before its shift begins. Rubbish in the Old City, including that of the monasteries and their schools, is usually dumped in the streets. Any removable bin, it is said, would be stolen. Workers here use their hands and brooms. Anshmister demonstrates the correct use of the broom — brisk forehand, not weary backhand. When the discussion ends, the local manager, Mr Chevsi, delivers his own address. Chevsi is an ex-schoolteacher who, municipal duties apart, writes poetry in an exercise book which he keeps in the drawer of his desk.

Chevsi's speech, delivered in elegant Arabic, is on democracy. All over the Western world, he informs the sanitation workers, the ideas of democracy have been proven false. There is no such thing as equality. People may have equal opportunities, but eventually an élite emerges. The machinery of society works best when everyone knows his place. Just as stairs must be swept from top to bottom, in order not to expend useless energy, decisions must be made at the top. Let those who envy the commanders, the men who give orders, reflect that it is they who bear the responsibility, they who are held to account, when things go wrong.

The little group of grizzled men and young boys, digital watches glinting on their deeply engrimed wrists, listen impassively. The speech is a soliloquy, not a subject for debate. When it is over, they file out into the alley. Mr Chevsi's view of the Mayor in the great chain of being is simple: 'Teddy Kollek is our father.'

Most of these early morning workers – 40 per cent of the total work-force of Arab Jerusalem – depend on Israel for their daily bread; and for these people, Kollek's role is purely paternalistic – particularly since they are not represented on the City Council by their own people. But there is another side to life in east Jerusalem, a population about whose future the professional 'Arab experts' make educated guesses, and whose relations with Israel are less intimate. This is the Palestinian élite: the old Jerusalem families like the Nusseibehs, the El Husseinis, the Dajanis; and Hebronite families like the El Khatibs (among them

the last governor and mayor of Jerusalem under Jordanian rule);
and there is also the new generation of professional people – doctors,
lawyers, journalists and teachers. Many of the sons and daughters
of the Jerusalem élite study in the universities of the surrounding
Arab states, and maintain a close relationship with Hussein's court
in Amman. Others are more closely identified with the PLO. Officially,
Israel tends to cultivate the first group, where possible, and watch
the second carefully. Differences of allegiance means that there is
no one Palestinian leadership in the city, but both hold nationalist
beliefs, and hope for a separate state, whether federated with Jordan
or independent.

For the workers of the city and, to a lesser extent, the merchant
class, Kollek's authority is unchallenged. The Palestinian élite is
another question altogether. Many have grown up, or come to matur-
ity, under Israeli rule. They have – consciously or unconsciously –
been stimulated by the example of Israeli freedoms, and resent all
the more their subordination to Israeli sovereignty. Education has
meant political consciousness, and a far more deeply rooted hostility
than is to be found among the village *mukhtars*, some of whom can
recall the British regime, or officials of Chevsi's type who see it as
politic to adjust to the new regime. A few of the younger professionals
are prepared for their own reasons to work with the municipality
and other Israeli institutions. There are east Jerusalem graduates of
Arab universities working in state schools where their salaries are
paid by Israel, in Israeli banking branches in east Jerusalem, and
in Israeli hospitals. The head of the Sheikh Jarrah clinic, Dr Nubani,
who qualified in Cairo and has his own private practice (like most
doctors in east Jerusalem), also works at the Jewish Shaarei Zedek
hospital, an orthodox foundation. Fuad Jaber, who works for the
Israeli Bank Leumi, has appeared on Israeli television to represent
east Jerusalem opinion.

Among the new Palestinian leadership, there are several men who
exchange political views with the Israelis. Hanna Siniora, the editor
of the east Jerusalem daily *Al Fajr* and the man who proposed to
head an independent Arab list at the next municipal elections, is
well known in Israeli left-wing circles, as is Dr Sari Nusseibeh of
Bir Zeit University, and appears regularly at meetings of the various
peace organizations; Siniora is also regularly summoned to the police

headquarters on various charges connected with the nationalist Palestinian policy advocated by his newspaper. All these people, and other men and women in less prominent positions but who also work side by side with Israelis, tread a very delicate course.

The idea of working within the Israeli system to achieve Palestinian political aims in fact originated with Sari Nusseibeh. He is the son of the late Palestinian leader Anwar Nusseibeh and a lecturer in Islamic Studies. During the past year Sari Nusseibeh has argued that after twenty years of occupation there is no sign that Israel is willing to allow the Palestinians independence. Thus the only course is to encourage the Israelis to annex the West Bank, and then for the Palestinians to demand equal political rights as Israeli citizens. Together with the present Israeli Arab population, the Palestinian Arabs would then constitute 40 per cent of the population of the country.

Siniora's proposal for an Arab municipal list was, in fact, the first attempt to put Nusseibeh's ideas to the test. Nusseibeh himself rejected the move, warning that it would reinforce Israel's attempt to separate the Jerusalem issue from that of the rest of the West Bank. Siniora argues that Jerusalem must be the initial project for an Israeli/Palestinian peace, 'the mother of any political solution', rather than 'the last item on the agenda'.

But Siniora's proposal of dual sovereignty is unacceptable to virtually all Israelis. Whilst Siniora has had many contacts with leading figures in Israel's Labour movement (he was at one time accepted both by Peres and by Arafat as an acceptable member of a Jordanian–Palestinian delegation at a potential peace conference), Kollek regards him as one of those Arabs 'who speak only for themselves'. The two men have never discussed the Jerusalem issue together. They have only met once briefly at the American consulate, but have attended some of the same social occasions. Siniora says of Kollek: 'We stand as two opposite sides. Kollek projects good intentions but denies the Palestinians the right to sovereignty. I stand for equality and parity.'

Siniora's view of the municipal political scene is somewhat bizarre. He sees potential allies among the secular moderate Jews of Jerusalem on the one side, or on the other, among the ultra-orthodox, whom he believes would support him in exchange for concessions on religious issues. For instance, he thinks he could ultimately promise them a complete stoppage of traffic in east Jerusalem on the Jewish Sabbath. This, however, could only reinforce the fears of those Jews, including Kollek, who fear 'a non-Zionist majority in the capital of Israel'. As to Kollek's frequent warnings that an Arab who co-operates with Israel courts death from terrorist action, Siniora says: 'If I am risking danger anyway [by his contacts with Jewish leaders] then let it be with the aim of bringing peace to the area. I believe that the only way of doing so is to change the present situation.'

Other leading politicians in Jerusalem are more openly hostile, or more cautiously co-operative. Feisal el Husseini, head of the Arab Studies Centre and a member of the Supreme Moslem Council, sees Kollek as 'the representative of the occupation of Jerusalem'. Like many other prominent Palestinians, Husseini believes that the central problem of Jerusalem is political and that the welfare of the city cannot be discussed from any other viewpoint. 'Kollek is cleverer than other potential mayors because he is good at public relations and because he isn't an extremist. He presents himself as mayor of a city open to three religions, but in fact he is a Zionist and serves Zionist interests, which are opposed to ours. My grandfather was mayor of Jerusalem at the beginning of the century, and now a "minority department" looks after me.' He acknowledges the improvements carried out in Jerusalem but attributes them to 'technology', not municipal policy. He denies that Kollek is 'popular' in east Jerusalem, as some of Kollek's aides maintain. 'He's simply the authority, the man the *mukhtars* appeal to, the man who gets things done.'

Jiries Khoury is head of the Bar Association, the Palestinian lawyers' group which has not operated since 1967. He sits in his shabby office in Salah ed Din Street, next door to that of the ex-governor of Jerusalem, Anwar El Khatib, and gives free legal advice. He feels that Israel's policies of open bridges with Jordan, and the fact that Jerusalem Arabs have their own press and vote for the municipality, are all part of a clever policy to allow the residents of the city 'to let off steam'. Like Husseini, he does not accept Kollek's picture of the multi-ethnic city, each of whose groups lead a separate existence. This is not true, he says, of Arab Moslems and Christians: 'Perhaps historically we were separate; now we are united against the occupation.' He does not believe that the changes in Jerusalem are for the benefit of the Palestinians; what really counts, he says, is the expropriation of the land. That, he says, has shown the Israelis' real intentions.

Because of Husseini's links with the PLO, he is confined to Jerusalem and can not leave his house between dusk and dawn. In the spring of 1987 he served three months in 'administrative detention' (jail). Khoury has no contacts whatever with Israelis and, like many of the older professional people in the city, appears to live in perpetual mourning for his lost status and prosperity.

Fayek Barakat, head of the Chamber of Commerce in east Jerusalem for the last thirty years, handles most of the contacts between the Arab middle class and Israel, without which life would come to a standstill. The Chamber of Commerce is a quasi-official body which handles all the documents that pass between Jordan and Arab Jerusalem, providing notarial services – witnessing land sales, school leaving diplomas and other papers – for those who do business with Jordan or study there.

The Supreme Moslem Council, which under the mandate provided political leadership for Moslems under non-Moslem rule in Palestine, was revived shortly after 1967 and is the channel for international protest against Israel. The Chamber of Commerce conveys the views of the merchants and householders to the 'authorities': the government and the municipality.

Barakat and his colleagues meet the Mayor in person every three or four months. He also sends ideas and recommendations to Amnon Niv, the City Engineer, about planning in east Jerusalem's Arab districts. Recently he discussed with Kollek the city plan for the 'Seam' area near the Damascus Gate, at the heart of the Arab commercial centre. The planners wanted a certain block to be made into a park; the merchants wanted more shops, and Barakat says that Kollek agreed to his proposal. But the dominant tone is one of complaint: inadequate street lighting, roads and drains; a policy geared exclusively to Israeli interests and which, he says, discriminates against local merchants. Himself the manager of the only new hotel to be built in the eastern city since 1967, Barakat cites the thousands of hotel rooms built by Israel and its foreign investors while Arab hoteliers are denied expansion, despite the fact that 30 per cent of Jerusalem's tourists come over the bridges from Jordan. The merchants complain that Arab factory owners cannot compete with Israeli goods, just as the West Bank is Israel's captive market. The system of taxation, they argue, penalizes the Arab shopkeepers and householders.

The Salah ed Din merchants should be taxed at a lower rate than those in Jaffa Road, they argue, as their sales are less; the municipality answers that they have the advantage of Saturday sales. Barakat says that the system of charging rates according to floor space penalizes the Arab householders who live in more spacious accommodation than the Israelis, with their blocks of flats. Inevitably, the bottom line in these arguments is political: Israel discriminates against the Arabs, say the Palestinians; the Palestinians have profited from Israeli rule, retort the Israelis, and point to higher income and welfare benefits. But these favour primarily the working class – one more argument against Israel in middle-class eyes.

Kollek has very little contact with the Palestinian élite, and he does not regard them as partners in a political dialogue. 'They speak only for themselves,' he says. Asked where the young men and women now graduating in their thousands from high schools in Jerusalem are going to find work in the city, he pauses; then he says, 'Many of them are leaving.' He adds that the city employs Arab engineers, runs professional courses, and that in the West Bank, too, Arab graduates are out of work.

Relations between Jews and Arabs in the city have changed since 1967. Immediately after the war, the Jews were in a state of euphoria, the Arabs in a state of shock; many Jews assumed – wrongly – that the Arabs were resigned to Israeli rule, and the Arabs assumed – wrongly again – that the situation was temporary. Both sides were curious to learn more about the other and there was a brief dialogue, soon silenced by the realities of the situation. The early months saw a tug of war between the Israeli government and the Palestinians. The government was faced with a series of legal anomalies: under existing Israeli law, the Palestinians were 'absentees' in their own homes; this was altered to make them 'residents of foreign nationality'.

They could not, under Israeli law, practise their trades or professions; the law was amended in order to enable them to do so. When they refused to apply for Israeli licences, the law was again amended to enable them to practise without applying. In most other respects, however, Israeli law was applied to them as if they were Israeli Arab citizens; they were sent regular tax demands and the education ministry insisted that the children in municipal state schools – about 60 per cent of all their schoolchildren – should study according to the Israeli Arab curriculum, which included lessons on Hebrew poets and Zionist ideology. Half the parents immediately withdrew their children and sent them to fee-paying private schools run by the churches and missions.

Nine months after the unification of the city, in February 1968, Kollek gave a talk to an audience of government officials on how not to treat the Arabs in the city. He told them that they had done everything wrong: they had moved into east Jerusalem, he said, as if it were just another Israeli town, sending tax demands and ordinances in Hebrew, making the Arabs queue for days, men and women together (against their customs), for identity cards and other documents. 'Some people seem to think that if we make it hard for them, they'll leave,' he said. 'Believe me, they won't.' The Arabs were just as attached to Jerusalem as the Jews, Kollek told them, perhaps more so; he had encountered old people who had given up American pensions and returned to Jerusalem to end their days there. He also attacked what he called 'the unspoken intention of turning the Arabs of the city into second-class citizens'. That, he said, would rebound on Israel itself. These were not the Arabs of 1948, villagers and peasants abandoned by their leaders. There were in Jerusalem ex-cabinet ministers and members of the Jordanian parliament, 'people who had sent their children to Oxford and Cambridge'.

Under Kollek, and with Meron Benvenisti's guidance, the municipality took a different line. Special contracts were drawn up with all the municipal employees of the Jordanian City Hall save for the legal counsellor – who had joined the other lawyers in boycotting Israel entirely – and their pension rights under Jordanian law were honoured. Kollek extended credit to merchants deprived of their livelihood and extracted a promise from the Prime Minister, Levi Eshkol, to compensate those he had evicted from the Moors Quarter. In all cases, Kollek presented the government with a *fait accompli* and then forced it to reimburse him.

According to a top civil servant who was party to all the administrative amendments governing the lives of Arabs in east Jerusalem –

amendments designed to enable them to live with the Israeli regime without unnecessary frictions – almost every one was put through after determined lobbying by Kollek himself. Many of these compromises were designed by Benvenisti, but it was Kollek who provided the political muscle to put them across. Thus the Wakf was allowed to take over the administration of the Temple Mount, Arabs were employed by special contract as foreign citizens who did not have to take the oath of loyalty to the state, and taxation was introduced only gradually, the 'defence levy' component never specifically appearing on the Arab tax forms.

Where Kollek was notably unsuccessful was in the matter of compensation to those thousands of Arabs who had abandoned property in west Jerusalem during the battles of 1948. Only in 1972, six years after the reunification of the city, was a joint office set up by the Finance and Justice Ministries to implement the law of compensation for 'absentee property'. But by December 1975, only eleven requests had been submitted, and only five of those by east Jerusalem Arabs – each of which represented several owners. Almost all withdrew their claims when they realized the absurdly low level of compensation envisaged, compared with the bureacratic trials of applying. The official in charge calculated that the owners would get 10 per cent or less of the real value of their property; and then asked to be relieved of his post after the final date for submission of claims, as he regarded the entire procedure as damaging to Israel's reputation. The official attitude was that there was no reason why Arabs should profit from the rise in land values during the years of Israeli rule.

Another issue, on which Kollek ultimately won his point after a long struggle, was the right of the city's Arabs to educate their children according to the Jordanian curriculum. The Ministry of Education at first resisted any suggestion that an 'enemy' programme be adopted. Kollek finally convinced them that the pupils who studied under the Israeli system were incapable subsequently of pursuing their education and careers in the Arab world. In 1976 the Ministry gave in where the higher classes in secondary schools were concerned, with the addition of lessons in Hebrew and civics. Though after 1977 a right-wing government was in power, the system was gradually extended to all pupils in state schools. By 1978, the state schools were once more attracting a substantial proportion of Arab children; today, of the number accounted for, about 40 per cent (of 45,000) study there, 42 per cent in private schools, and 9 per cent in refugee schools run by UNWRA.

On the face of it, allowing Arab children to follow the Jordanian curriculum is an extraordinarily liberal measure. It is also in the interests of those who want to keep Jerusalem under Israel's control. The children are educated in state schools under official supervision, and what they learn enables them to qualify for universities and jobs in the Arab world, which may also encourage their ultimate emigration.

In the business and commercial sector, Arab banks in the city remained closed; this was chiefly because the Arab negotiators wanted them to function openly as branches of the central banks in Amman. Though an Arab bank recently reopened in Nablus, the idea of a Jordanian branch in Jerusalem was too much for Israel. Banking functions were soon taken over by the 'money changers' still visible everywhere in east Jerusalem. They trade in both Israeli and Jordanian currency (though this is illegal in the west of the city). The Chamber of Commerce, moreover, serves as the channel through which Jordanian money is paid out to individuals and institutions in the city, including those teachers and lawyers and other state employees who refuse to work with the Israelis.

All these arrangements took time to emerge, and during that time both Israel and the Jerusalem Arabs learned some hard lessons. For most of the period, between late July 1967 and September 1970, Jerusalem was a city in which attempts at civil rebellion, as well as terror, were met with severe repression. Groups of Palestinians formed quasi-political bodies, organized strikes, refused to pay taxes and appealed to the outside world for help. The heads of the political movements were deported, the strikes broken and demonstrations dispersed with a joint show of force, both by the army – there were paratroopers in the streets – and the police. During the same period, the first wave of terror against the Jewish civilian population began, with bombs placed in residential areas and cinemas, restaurants and markets. The Israeli security forces succeeded in infiltrating the terrorist networks and quickly demolished one after another; meanwhile, the borders with Jordan were sealed. (Before this, Yasser Arafat was actually operating out of Nablus, in the West Bank.) Local support for the terrorists was suppressed by the destruction of houses whose inhabitants had sheltered them, or where they had lived with their families.

Finally, Hussein's destruction of PLO forces in Jordan in what came to be known as 'Black September', in 1970, crippled Palestinian efforts to organize an effective terror base in Jordan. Bombs were still placed in public places, but terror became increasingly sporadic, disorganized and amateur in execution. There was now little chance to smuggle in arms from outside the West Bank – though some Israeli army explosives and grenades reached the terrorists via the Jewish criminal underworld.

Although there are no official figures on the dead and wounded by Arab terrorist action in Jerusalem over the last twenty years, authoritative sources put those killed at just under a hundred. A report published recently in the leading *Haaretz* daily newspaper listed seventeen killed (five of them tourists) and 287 wounded between January 1980 and January 1987. During the same period, three Arabs were killed in reprisals by Jews.

Kollek's arguments that collective punishments were counterproductive had little weight with the army; but in a committee formed specifically to deal with security and civil rebellion, headed by the chief of the local police force, Saul Rosolio, Kollek was more successful. From August 1969 the demolition of houses in Jerusalem was discontinued, though strikes were still 'discouraged' by the police and demonstrations broken up.

The first terrorist attacks were followed by violence against Jerusalem Arabs by Jewish youths, mainly from the old frontier districts, who chased and beat up Arab passers-by after each incident and tried to force their way into Arab districts to take revenge. Police, government and city all acted immediately, and strongly, to condemn them. The police protected the Arab districts and both Kollek and Moshe Dayan, then Minister of Defence and at the height of his popularity, called the youths 'hooligans whose behaviour was the same as co-operation with the Fatah terrorists'. This had its effect; though even more serious bomb attacks by terrorists followed, there was no further reaction.

Nothing has embittered the Jews of Jerusalem against the Arabs more than Palestinian terrorists who have operated sporadically in the city since 1967. Most of the more serious incidents took place during the three years following the Six Day War: among them, bombs set off in the Jewish wholesale market of Mahane Yehuda and others placed in cinemas, supermarkets, a university cafeteria and in crowded buses. Explosives have been located in cars parked in central streets of the western city, in an old refrigerator left on a pavement at Zion Square, in dustbins, shopping bags and even in hollowed-out watermelons and loaves of bread. Unlike the incident at the Dung Gate in September 1986, almost all were designed to kill or terrorize civilians.

Although the security forces managed to round up members of terrorist cells almost as rapidly as they were formed, and the danger diminished significantly after September 1970, terror left its mark on Jerusalem. Police were sent to schools to instil caution into children from an early age – charts displayed in school corridors showed the variety of explosives used and the ruses to watch for. Every school in Jewish areas of the city organizes four-hour stints of guard duty mandatory for parents at least once yearly, and several times a year if more than one child in the family attended the school. The first shift of parents is supposed to check out the school grounds and each classroom in the building; conscientious parents even check lavatory cisterns and classroom cupboards. The second shift continues to watch the school gates until the end of school hours – usually at 2 p.m. These arrangements are usually amateurish – the parents patrol armed with nothing more lethal than knitting needles – but the general purpose is deterrent.

Because of the danger of bombs placed under seats and on racks in buses, all bus drivers were ordered to inspect buses before they set out from each terminal. But as it proved impossible to check every passenger boarding during the rush hours (sometimes by the exits), several Jews, among them schoolchildren, have been killed or wounded by explosions on buses.

Security officials still check bags and parcels at the entrance to the city's main department stores, at cinemas, theatres and concert halls as a matter of routine. Civilians are alert, and any abandoned briefcase or packet is suspect. In post offices, stickers are attached to parcels requesting the recipients to check the sender's name and address before opening them. Waste baskets have disappeared from lampposts. The routine civil defence and border police patrols in the city, which frequently stop Arab passers-by and check their documents, are also deterrent measures much resented by the Arab population. Another effect of sporadic attacks on Jews is a boom in the sale of small arms — many civilians who serve in the army reserves keep revolvers in homes, cars and offices. But as the vast majority of terrorist attacks have been the surreptitious planting of explosives, not open violence, there have been very few shoot-outs in the city streets.

In recent years, the security forces have proved so successful in preventing the import of explosives and arms over the Jordan bridges (the result both of Jordanian co-operation and exhaustive checks at the bridges themselves), that most recent acts of terror, or of anti-Jewish violence, have been carried out with knives rather than bombs or even revolvers. Yet, paradoxically, fear and anger against Arab terrorists, and the identification of Arabs as potential terrorists, has been expressed more readily by certain sections of the Jerusalem population over the last few years.

There are several possible reasons for this. After twenty years, acts of terror in the city remind Israelis of Arab hostility to their rule — a factor many would like to deny or ignore. The argument often heard in bus queues and in shops, or each time a suspect package is checked and a crowd gathers, that 'Arabs can go wherever they like in the city unharmed, whereas we have to watch out for bombs or get stabbed if we go shopping in the Old City', sidesteps politics.

Secondly, there has been no concerted condemnation of terror by leading Palestinians in the city. It is only very recently that a few distinguished Arab intellectuals have spoken out against political violence of all kinds. A catalogue published recently by *Al Fajr* for its English edition lists all bomb outrages under 'Resistance'.

Thirdly: the political view put forward by the right-wing parties in recent years that the Arabs are in Jerusalem on sufferance — and that their presence is conditional on their good behaviour — has encouraged counter terror by marginal Jewish goups unknown before the 1980s.

Thus while the physical threat to safety in the city has actually diminished, fear has spread to Arab civilians as well. Both sides now fear the consequences of an explosion in the city, and assume the worst when a jet plane overhead breaks the sound barrier, or the 'robot' – a long-range defusing device – races through the streets into action.

Relations between Jews and Arabs in the city have settled into a formal pattern. The tensions are never far below the surface. The Arab minority remain nationals of an enemy state, ruled by Israel against their will. The Jewish majority is made up of men and women of whom most have served in the army. Some two thousand families in the capital have lost men in one of Israel's five wars; many of those over forty emigrated from Arab countries in which they were in some ways second-class citizens, and they resent precisely that common background they share with the Arabs. In recent years fanatical right-wing groups have emerged, one headed by Meir Kahana, a man who serves in the Knesset and whose position gives a spurious legitimacy to his racist speeches.

Yet despite all this, Jerusalem is generally a tranquil city, supporting Kollek's claim that people of different ethnic groups can coexist peacefully even when riven by political conflict. Kollek's own policies have done much to reduce tensions; but there are other factors as well. Jerusalem is still a semi-rural city where the anonymity which helps criminals is difficult to find. The shabbiness of Arab Jerusalem is partly misleading; much money is funnelled into the city not only by Jordan but also by the PLO and Saudi Arabia. The living standards of the working class have risen dramatically since 1967, despite the rise in the cost of living. While prosperity has not eliminated political feeling, it has made strikes, demonstrations and violence less attractive, particularly since Arab Jerusalem is so dependent on tourism.

Even attempts to organize 'non-violent' protest have been rarely successful. Mubarak Awad, a Christian Palestinian psychologist influenced by Gandhi and the Quakers, who runs a non-violence centre in east Jerusalem, gives several reasons for this: private schools connected with the churches discourage political action; there is no Jerusalem university to foster activism among the young; and resistance is difficult to organize in the comfortably off Jerusalem middle class. Another deterrent to protest is rough handling of demonstrators by the police and the army, which, as Kollek told the Chief of Staff, Mordechai Gur, in 1976, could 'separate the city into two rival camps', but which undoubtedly discourages many from taking to the streets.

For all these reasons, Jerusalem, since the 1970s, has been peaceful. Yet the presence of Arabs and Jews on one another's territory is always something to be explained, praised or condemned; never something natural, to be taken for granted.

The united city is visibly the home of two very different peoples, with different languages, religions and cultures. This is clear not only from the street signs, the newspapers, the placards, and the different costumes of various communities – all those things which lend the most obvious 'colour' to a multi-ethnic city; but from the appearance of the newer Jewish and Arab districts. Jews live in apartment blocks, and their suburbs are clearly the combined effort of teams of surveyors, architects and decorators. Arabs live in villas with wide verandas and gardens, or in cottages each with its little patch of land and trellised vines, in villages built with haphazard winding alleys, paths and steps. The traditional style of Arab houses, with their large, central guest room and separate quarters for women, is entirely foreign to Jewish Israelis; so is the idea of a family house in which the father may live on the ground floor and his children – in order of seniority – above him. Israelis live in a bureaucratic universe in which homes are 'housing units' distributed by ministries; the Arabs in a hierarchic world in which one family parcels out its land among its children.

The distinctiveness of the two Jerusalems is not just the result of their separate development. Here, everything is separate: not only districts, and houses and schools, but bus lines, and bloodbanks, and fire brigades. It would be at least theoretically possible for a Jew and an Arab to pass their entire lives, from birth in separate hospitals to death and burial in separate cemeteries, without ever coming into contact. The way in which Israel has developed its suburbs has broken the old division between west-Jewish and east-Arab Jerusalem, but the road system between Jewish districts has been planned to avoid the Arab districts, for 'security reasons'. Everything underlines the basic contradiction in the 'pluralist' city: that to preserve so complete a separation between the two communities is also to reinforce their suspicions and fears of one another.

What brings the two together is mainly commercial interest. During the day, and especially on Saturdays, when shops in Jewish Jerusalem are closed, Jews and Arabs buy and sell in the two commercial centres of the town. A handful of shops in west Jerusalem carries signs in Arabic; in the Old City and east Jerusalem, most of the stall owners and shopkeepers speak Hebrew. In fact, most Arabs who work or deal with Jews have learned Hebrew, while few Jews have found it necessary to learn Arabic – a clear sign, among others, of which group dominates the city.

Jewish car owners take their cars to be serviced at Arab garages, where it is cheaper; others patronize Arab carpenters and craftsmen, for the same reason. While wealthy Arabs crowd the waiting-rooms of specialists in the Jewish hospitals, many Jews patronize Arab dentists and gynaecologists, who charge as little as a third of the Jewish prices. Arabs buy electrical appliances made in Israel, synthetic carpets and fashionable clothes from the Jews. Jews buy 'oriental' souvenirs, Bedouin carpets and embroidered dresses from the Arabs.

When Jews and Arabs visit one another's districts on their day off, it is as tourists. Arab families go to the Biblical Zoo and the Israel Museum, and picnic in the parks in the west of the city; boys roller skate on Saturday evenings in the Liberty Bell Garden. At first, the boys visited the swimming-pools in west Jerusalem, but with the introduction of membership subscriptions in the hotel and kibbutz pools, swimming was too dear for many, including Arab boys. This year, even the Jerusalem Pool (a general facility but now privately run) was declared open only to subscribers and their guests. There is little fraternization. A British Jew who has visited Israel more than twenty-five times since 1971 (once for an eight-month period) has never seen, at the home of his dozens of Israeli friends, a single Arab guest – even though three of his friends are university experts on Arab affairs. At dusk, most visits end. Arabs are rarely seen in the Jewish concert halls and theatres, and only tourists visit the little bars in east Jerusalem – mainly in hotels, for Moslems drink no alcohol; Israeli cinemas show no films dubbed or subtitled in Arabic. On summer nights, however, both Jews and Arabs patronize what is perhaps the only meeting-place in the city: the watermelon stalls in the former no man's land near the Damascus Gate, one of which is jointly owned by local Jews and Arabs. Clients squat on wooden stools, eat the freshly sliced fruit and drink *sahleb*, the Arab gruel seasoned with cinnamon and raisins, and watch cassettes of Rambo, Bruce Lee and Ninja on the flickering video sets. Some Jewish boys bring their girls; Arab girls never go out unchaperoned. After midnight, the cassettes are exchanged and the few remaining clients huddle round to watch the porn. Elsewhere in the city, Jewish and Arab fences swop parts from stolen cars and other stolen property. Jewish prostitutes do business for Arab pimps. Drug pedlars, who have always profited from the reopening of the ancient trade route between Egypt and Israel, do business on both sides. But this is done behind the walls. The only signs of the Arab presence in the western city in the small hours are the charcoal and wood stoves, brought to warm the Arab watchmen at the Jewish building sites, glowing and redolent until the morning.

The two populations know very little of what goes on in one another's sector of town. A recent survey indicated that apart from the main landmarks in the centre, Jewish and Arab children could not identify roads or buildings 'on the other side'. The René Cassin secondary school in one of the newer suburbs, Ramat Eshkol, lies a bare hundred yards from the Abdulla Bin Hussein school in Sheikh Jarrah, yet neither was aware of the other's existence. The municipality organized two hundred meetings between Jewish and Arab young people – without publicity – between 1967 and 1972. But recently, chiefly because of opposition from the orthodox factions in the city, who fear contact between Jewish girls and Arab boys, such meetings have become rarer. The Foundation runs music and art groups for all children.

The municipal education department head, Michael Gal, has tried to bring together Jewish and Arab teachers in the city: at the first meeting, forty Arabs arrived and thirty Jews; by the second, the Jewish numbers had dropped to five. A more recent effort led to the Arab teachers' cancellation. At the Hebrew University, almost the only Arab students are Israeli Arabs from elsewhere in the country; Jerusalem Arabs have their own colleges and universities, mostly in the West Bank. Because of the lack of housing in Arab Jerusalem, many of the Israeli Arab students have looked for rooms for rental in Jewish Jerusalem; but whether for fear of terrorists, or other reasons (which in the nature of things are seldom spelled out), they often do not find them and, when they do, are often subject to harassment or actual violence.

The almost total separation of Arab and Jewish districts means that there is little awareness among the Jews of the problems of Arab neighbours who may live only a few hundred yards away. The design of the new suburbs, whose walls and highways cut them off effectively from the villages, makes this even more pronounced.

But recently, in East Talpiot, a group of residents organized a protest on behalf of their next door village, Sur Bahir. Sur Bahir faces East Talpiot across a valley in which the villagers have many fields and orchards. In 1970, the Israel Lands Authority expropriated over five hundred acres from the village, most of which was used for the construction of the Jewish suburb. The land that was left continued to serve the villagers who grew olives, almonds and other crops there to supplement their income. In 1985, the Jewish National Fund, which handles Israel's afforestation projects, sent in tractors and began uprooting the crops and trees the villagers had most recently planted. The area, they explained, was scheduled for a national park surrounding Jerusalem. Arab trees were to be uprooted to make room for Jewish trees – olives and almonds for pine trees.

The villagers challenged the state's right to take agricultural land for parkland, arguing that it had been expropriated for a residential area. The case went up to the Supreme Court. The villagers lost, but not before they had enlisted support from the East Talpiot community organization – one of those set up in the new suburbs to encourage local involvement in municipal affairs.

The JNF, with municipal support, proposed a compromise. But the villagers refused at first to haggle over what they still maintained was their own land. Meanwhile tractors moved in and freshly planted olive trees were uprooted, pine saplings planted.

On a cold February afternoon in 1987, Jewish and Arab neighbours held a demonstration on the disputed hillside. On the crest of the hill behind them was the ruin of a Jewish emplacement dating from 1948, the Bell outpost. A few yards away was a small grove of trees, curved towards the city by the fierce western winds, surrounded by a makeshift barbed-wire fence; the warning sign 'Danger! Mines' was written in three languages: Hebrew, Arabic and English. Twenty years after the last war, the mined orchard has still not been cleared by the army.

Arab demonstrators carried placards: 'Expropriation is not the way to peace'; 'Return our Land. Aren't 2,000 dunams enough'; and – a message to the municipality – 'Land taken, 2,000 dunams; services provided – o'. During this demonstration, which involved only the villagers and a small group of East Talpiot residents (most of them from America and England), the Mayor arrived. His Sierra bumped down the muddy hillside; he got out, said a few words expressing the hope that justice would be done so that Jews and Arabs could work together for coexistence, and was warmly applauded. After he left, the village *mukhtar* announced that Kollek intended to take up the issue with the Minister of Agriculture (a Labour man, but a confirmed hawk on territorial questions), and there was scattered applause. Two little girls from the Jewish suburb and the Arab village 'planted' an olive sapling in a plastic pail; the last speaker at the demonstration said: 'All this is part of the wider Palestinian problem which began forty years ago; each obstacle removed, like this, is a step towards its solution.' Few observers were as optimistic. Kollek and the Minister finally reached an agreement by which the forestry commission would plant not pine, oak and other non fruit-bearing trees, but olive trees, which the Sur Bahir villagers would be allowed to cultivate. As a special gesture to the villagers Kollek persuaded the commission to plant – in anticipation of the usual planting season – some sixty mature olive trees. Yet the whole area remains subject to ad hoc decisions by minor officials and the villagers have no legal say over what happens to their land, though while Kollek remains mayor he may extract concessions.

Eight villages, as well as land taken from twenty-eight villages in all, were added to Israeli Jerusalem in 1967. Though they provide much of the labour force for the modern city, they belong in a different world – that of the rural West Bank. Some are peasant villages long settled by the sedentary *fellahin*. Others are Bedouin settlements which have taken root around the city over the past hundred and fifty years. All have their own territorial logic. Some cultivate orchards in the valleys between the Jerusalem hills; others cling near the watershed line on the precipitous, bare hills leading down to the Judean desert. Most lost land to the city during the mass expropriations of the late 1960s and early 1970s; that alone would have been enough to send thousands looking for work in the city, where the wages are higher than those paid in Arab centres. But in any case many of the sons of the leading clans had already left to work in the Persian Gulf and the neighbouring Arab states, sending money back regularly to their families, seldom losing touch.

To take the municipal services to these villages is even more difficult than serving the ready-made satellite suburbs of the Ministry of Housing. Most of the villages have dirt tracks rather than roads, where the houses, nestling in the hillsides, are inaccessible to municipal trucks. The style of building – with rooms and outhouses added as the need arises – is such that it is hard to control, licence or check on 'illegal' additions.

The villages are so close to the city that flocks of goats often pasture off the hedges of suburban gardens or parks, guided by shepherd boys. Donkeys carry the villagers' fodder home, and brilliantly caparisoned camels are stationed outside the Intercontinental Hotel on the Mount of Olives. Yoel Marinov, of the Urban Improvement Department, and Tommy Sadeh, chief veterinarian, detect a threat to city health. In 1970 there was a cholera outbreak in Jerusalem, the first in many years, traced to vegetables grown by villagers with sewage water. Recently, in a valley near one of the new suburbs, inspectors found that a manhole had been blocked and water diverted. One morning in September 1986, Marinov sent out inspectors with a police escort to stop a village party bringing their produce into town without permits. Sadeh is concerned by the threat of rabies; jackals and the yellow desert dogs who roam the West Bank often come out of the wilderness and bite domestic animals in the city. After a four-year campaign, he has pushed through a new by-law which will prevent villagers bringing their animals into the city without a permit. One group of Bedouins who give camel rides to tourists could not at first find a company which would insure their clients against falls and bites. It took some time for the licensing bureau to accept camels as 'vehicles'.

The Arabs argue indignantly that all this is intended just to penalize and contain the villagers; Marinov and Sadeh that it is a necessary precaution in a modern city. At all events, the sheep market opposite the Rockefeller Museum will soon be a memory, and there will be no more goats roaming the suburban streets, and no Bedouin women sitting outside the Holy Sepulchre selling parsley and mint – unless they can produce a licence.

The proximity of the villages to Jerusalem has bred a taste for consumer goods, and the new political reality has encouraged the determination to stay put and consolidate those lands which remain. Both factors affect the look of the villages today. Israeli-made solar heaters and television aerials share the flat rooftops with harvests of nuts and fruit laid out to dry. Older women, wearing traditional Bedouin embroidered dresses, walk as far as ten miles into Jerusalem in the early morning to sell figs, grapes and vegetables, carried on flat, hard cushions on their heads; some work as cleaning women in Jewish households. Many of the younger women, however, who now wear a *chador*-style Moslem headdress over their modern clothes, study in the West Bank universities. There are doctors and architects in these villages, as well as peasants. And though most of the villagers now work in the city, any land which can be farmed is swiftly planted. Even the beautiful, sculptured terraces on the hill-sides, some abandoned since Byzantine times, are now being re-claimed; for, above all, the villagers fear the loss of more of their land and they know that once cultivated, land is rarely taken.

Of all the villages on the periphery of Jerusalem, Bet Sefafa has probably suffered most. Between 1948 and 1967, it was half in Israel, half in Jordan, with – from the 1950s – a fence down the centre. The railway line between Jerusalem and Tel Aviv, which winds through the Judean hills, ran just parallel to the frontier, inside Israel. A pretty village with walled streets, and many orchards and gardens, Bet Sefafa was reunited only to be amputated from all sides. To the north, even before 1967, part of its land had been taken for a Jewish suburb, Patt. Soon after the war, more lands were expropriated to the south for the suburb of Gilo. Finally, a six-lane highway, crossing the village by an overpass but with no exit to the village itself, joined Patt and Gilo.

During the early days after the war, a group of American orthodox Jews invaded the village and set up their own colony, profiting from Jordanian laws which had prevented the registration of unfinished houses in the owners' names. They took over a number of such houses, promising to complete the building, and then refused to vacate them when their lease was up. In the subsequent legal battles, the villagers won back only a few of their houses.

Bet Sefafa has never given Israel any trouble, and in 1974, before the elections, Kollek admitted that he had a 'bad conscience' about the low level of municipal facilities in the village. Nevertheless, it was not until 1980 that a sewerage system was introduced in the village, which still has no health clinic of its own, no kindergarten, and no community centre – though it does have its own sports club: the village was champion of the West Bank football teams in 1978. Those who can afford it send their children to private schools in east Jerusalem, complaining of the low standards of the local school. The village also lacks proper roads, pavements and the facilities of the nearby Jewish suburbs.

A group of young families led by Mussa Elian – an Israeli Arab who runs a tax advisory and insurance agency in east Jerusalem – banded together to organize a joint housing project. Kollek and his team prodded the Housing Ministry, which helped with mortgage facilities, and the Lands Authority, which lowered the price of public land available in the village, and helped them build a specially designed complex at the centre. In some senses, the problems of Bet Sefafa are those of any village community engulfed by a spreading city. But not quite: though the village has never staged a violent demonstration, let alone harboured terrorists, security agents frequently visit it and take suspects for identity parades.

Kollek's own relations with the Arabs of the city function on two levels. The élite know how to find their way round the corridors of power; for the rest, there is the Arab Affairs Advisor, the liaison officer who is the city's fuse box for all complaints and problems. At election times, Kollek's faction has its own network of relationships in the poorer districts of Jerusalem and the villages, mostly through the clan heads, the *mukhtars* and other public figures. During the first elections after the war, in 1969, contacts were developed through those members of the Jordanian municipality who continued to work for Israel, and the *mukhtars* were consulted as to the optimum use of the budgets allotted to the Arab sector of the city. A token fee was paid to the *mukhtars* for their co-operation, following the practice of earlier, colonial governments, and it soon became clear to the villagers that those who co-operated with the municipal authorities would not lose by it. Though many observers doubted that any Arab would appear at the polling booths, at the first elections eight thousand valid votes were registered, which meant that 15 per cent of those eligible had turned out. (Under the Jordanian regime, only property owners had voted and women did not vote at all.) Almost all were votes for Kollek. The proportion of those voting rose during subsequent elections to something like 20 per cent. In 1978 the election system was changed allowing for a separate, personal vote for the mayoral candidate, and during the 1978 and 1983 elections the Arab vote also gave Kollek two to three seats on the City Council; in 1983 these 13,000 votes were crucial, enabling him to retain a bare majority in the city forum.

The only man among the Jerusalem Arab élite who maintained a relationship with Kollek, as an equal, was Anwar Nusseibeh, who was probably the most distinguished Arab leader to remain in the city after 1967. Ex-Jordanian Ambassador to London, and ex-Minister of Defence, Nusseibeh continued to play a leading role in city affairs, primarily as director of the largest industrial concern in east Jerusalem, the Electricity Corporation, but also as member of the family building firm which built the Nusseibeh Quarter, the only popular housing estate to rise in the city under Israeli rule, which – with some financial help from the Ministry of Housing – provided for many of the evacuees of the Jewish Quarter.

For all his Cambridge education and diplomatic experience in the service of Jordan, Nusseibeh was primarily a Palestinian patriot who, during the twenty years of occupation, became steadily more committed to the radical nationalist cause. But Kollek and Nusseibeh continued to talk. When Kollek speaks of Nusseibeh today, it is with none of the patronizing attitude he adopts towards the other 'notables' of the *ancien régime*.

The East Jerusalem Electricity Corporation may seem an odd choice for a political symbol, but it has become one of the key issues in preserving the peace in the city. The original, mandatory concession was formulated in symbolic terms, for its range was defined as 'twenty kilometres from the summit of the Rotunda of the Holy Sepulchre'. In the heady days of summer 1967, Kollek actually proposed nationalizing the firm; but the government disagreed, and the moment passed. Subsequently, over the years, Kollek helped the Corporation to remain in Arab hands, realizing how important this company was as a symbol of Palestinian independence.

When the new suburbs were set up in what was formerly Arab territory, the Israeli government was opposed to an Arab company supplying their current, but the law did not allow Israel to regard itself as Jordan's heir to the concession, and the new suburbs were duly linked to the Arab grid in January 1970. Extra generators were added, and bills sent out in Hebrew as well as Arabic. This was the first time that the Jewish suburbs, planned to be in all respects independent of the nearby Arab districts, had to rely on an Arab organization. Even the army base situated in the north-east of the city was serviced by the company.

The first problems were not political, but technical. The generators soon proved unable to deal not only with the Jews' consumption of electricity, but with the triple increase of electrical current used by Jerusalem's Arabs. By 1972 it was clear that the east Jerusalem company would be forced to buy current from the Israeli Electricity Corporation, and today, 95 per cent of the current is indeed bought from Israel.

As the company became increasingly dependent on Israel in the technical sense, political pressure built up, in Israel, for a takeover. There were frequent breakdowns in the supply (many because con-tractors working in the new suburbs inadvertently dug up cables) and increasingly unconvincing explanations of how they had hap-pened: dew damping a cable, Israeli soldiers 'sniping' at lines. There was no question of sabotage; the company was simply not equipped to handle the increased demand. Each time the lights went out, there were indignant protests by Jewish consumers and demands that the Arab concession be ended.

By this time the electricity supply had become a political issue, with Kollek and the municipality pleading for Arab independence and the Ministry of Energy pressing for a takeover. Protesters gathered outside Kollek's house angrily terming him 'Defender of Islam'. A High Court ruling in 1980 said that the government had the right to take over the concession in Jerusalem (but not in the West Bank, which stretches from Ramallah to Jericho), but also recommended that the government reconsider its decision. In 1981, Kollek, while reminding the Minister of Energy that he had himself originally recommended a takeover, said it was too late now. To end the concession prematurely would lead to international arbitration àt the Hague Court and again call in question the legitimacy of Israel's rule in Jerusalem. It would also, he pointed out, cost a fortune in compensation.

The government 'reconsidered'. But by the end of 1986, with the end of the concession now in sight, there were fresh pressures not to renew it. It was clear to the Israelis that the company was vastly overstaffed and its equipment inadequate; moreover, King Hussein, who had previously backed Nusseibeh to the hilt, now withdrew his backing, possibly because the latter's stand on Palestinian independence had become too uncompromising for the King's liking. Although Kollek several times warned the Israeli corporation that they might have to step in at any moment if the supply broke down, he nevertheless hesitated to recommend an outright takeover, not only because Israel would be faced with many of the same technical problems, but because a legal battle would increase political tensions in the city.

In late 1986, with Nusseibeh a gravely sick man, it was agreed that the Arab company would concede the new suburbs to the Israelis (despite the fact that they were still seen as being in Arab territory) but retain the districts inhabited by Arabs. However, in the spring of 1987 the Arab stand became less compromising and, concurrently, breakdowns of the electric current supplied by the East Jerusalem Electricity Corporation multiplied. By March 1987 irate crowds of Jewish householders were once more protesting outside the Mayor's house, and Kollek finally recommended in exasperation that the Minister of Energy, Moshe Shahal, should remove the Jewish districts from the Arab concession area. In June 1987 the Ministry formulated a compromise policy. The concession was to be extended by a further ten years. The East Jerusalem Corporation was to serve Arab districts only, the Israeli corporation – the Jewish. This solution was said to have been approved by Jordan. It remained to be seen whether a compromise would ultimately be found to save Arab face or whether this would become an open confrontation.

Apart from his powers as an arbitrator in such matters as the Electricity Corporation, Kollek has another semi-formal role between the

Arabs and the government: recommending who shall, and who shall not, return to Jerusalem from outside the areas under Israeli control – subject always to the agreement of the security people, who have the last word.

During the first months after the Six Day War, Israel (or rather Moshe Dayan, who decided all policy in the occupied territories) allowed most of the Arabs who had fled Jerusalem and the West Bank to return. The situation was more difficult for those who had left to study or work in the Arab states before the war and now wished to come home. Committees were set up to judge each case on its merits. A list of criteria was established: husbands could be reunited with wives, and if women were left alone, their menfolk were allowed back to look after them. But the criteria narrowed steadily and rapidly. If a marriage is undertaken now between a Jerusalem woman and a man living in Amman, it is the wife who must join her husband. There are today very few family reunions. As for travel abroad, the current regulations clearly favour those who visit the Arab states (via the Allenby Bridge across the Jordan) over those who visit Europe and America. The traveller east can stay abroad for three years on an Israeli *laissez-passer*, if an Arab state has not granted him permanent residence. The traveller going to the West, leaving from Ben Gurion airport, must renew his permit after one year at an Israeli consulate. If he obtains a work permit abroad (such as the American Green Card), he is disqualified from further residence in Jerusalem.

Officially all travel permits are the province of the Ministry of the Interior. But in May 1976, at a meeting between Kollek and the Minister of Justice, it was agreed that his own personal recommendations would carry special weight. Kollek's own criteria are influenced by what he considers to be the possible contribution by a returning Palestinian to the welfare of the city, as well as by humanitarian factors.

The office of the Mayor's Advisor on Arab Affairs is a counterpart of the similar offices in government departments, each of which, including the Prime Minister's Office, has its own 'Arab Department' – or, more tactfully, 'Minorities Department'. The middle class and the well connected bypass the office and deal directly with the Mayor and his aides. The Arab Advisor is the link between the rest of the Arabs and the City Engineer's office where building permits, demolition threats or property arguments are concerned; with the security people, after arbitrary arrests or detention; with the Interior Ministry, regarding permits to leave the country or return; with the Municipal Treasurer's office or the income tax authorities, when tax demands are resisted or cannot be paid; with the city maintenance experts, when poorly built houses are swamped with winter rain – and in a hundred other matters in which the Jewish resident of Jerusalem would seek out the department directly responsible.

Every Tuesday, Amir Cheshin, the current Advisor, sets out on his weekly round usually with one of his aides – like himself, an ex-official of the military government in the West Bank. One aide is an Arab contractor who until recently worked in a municipal position.

His first stop is to arbitrate between two neighbours in a dispute over a parapet one has built on a shared wall. Then he moves on to a house built on a slope overlooking Silwan, south of the Temple Mount. Here the newly installed sewage pipes cross a householder's land, and the householder objects. Though they were placed underground, he wants compensation, or a further reduction in taxes. The Israelis say he is a regular troublemaker, with three wives and twenty children.

Out north, on the road to Ramallah, Cheshin visits a newly built district of expensive villas; between them are unpaved roads, no more than dirt strips. None of the owners wants to give up land for a public garden or to contribute to the paving of the road. In the Jewish districts, when the Housing Ministry builds from scratch, it lays out the whole area as part of the package. In older districts, the tenants pay part of the cost.

At Issawiya, a village on the eastern slopes of Mount Scopus, Cheshin points to a four-storey building belonging to the owner of a business in east Jerusalem, built without a permit. At the lower level of the village, where winter rains drain into the valley, a working party recruited by the *mukhtar* is building a retaining wall; the city provides the materials, the village provides the labour: a familiar arrangement in the Arab districts, unknown in Jewish sectors. A similar system has been put to work in A Tur, the next stop on the tour, a village cascading down from the Mount of Olives into the Judean desert. Here, one of the new neighbourhood councils has been set up. It is not, as in the Jewish districts, run by its own tenants, but by a young Israeli Arab woman from a Galilee village, Wahiba Abu Ras, who has an MA in sociology from Haifa university. In this village, the residents contributed half the cost of a main sewer, received the rest from the municipality and a project organized by them with a Jewish charity abroad, and, with manholes, lids and pipes from the city, carried out the work themselves. Now, teams of village men are building flights of steps to link the village main roads and the houses far below. Abu Ras has persuaded the *mukhtar* to give some of his own land, deep in the valley, for a village park.

A Tur has a population of six thousand, most of whom are shop-keepers, labourers, taxi drivers and clerks in Arab hospitals. As in all the villages, the more successful have studied abroad and work in the Persian Gulf, Europe or America. One, a doctor now in Germany, with a foreign wife, wants to come back to the village; Kollek is dealing with the request. Abu Ras has changed the sanitation layout, helped set up a mother and child centre, and hopes to set up a community centre with money provided by Jordan and villagers who live abroad. Through sheer tenacity and obvious concern for the welfare of the village, she has managed to win the confidence of all three local *mukhtars*, despite the fact that she is a young unmarried woman with an Israeli education. She manoeuvres skilfully between the Mount of Olives Arab council – the local authority in Jordanian times – and the Israeli municipality. For contacts with Jordan she uses the stationery of the Mount of Olives council, and while she persuades the villagers to contribute to better services, she also educates them as to how best to confront the regulations on planning which have defeated so many other Arab contractors and house-holders.

The last stop on Cheshin's patrol leads through one of the Bedouin villages south of Jerusalem – Arab es Sawahra. He points out an alley, little more than a furrow in the side of the bare limestone cliff, where an illegally built house was recently destroyed by the municipal inspectors. 'How would anyone have known it was there?' he asks. 'Someone must have informed on his neighbour.' Here, the municipality recently built a new school, relieving some of the children of a walk across the hillsides to a school nearer the city.

The municipal truck skirts the Hill of Evil Counsel, the mandatory High Commissioner's Residence, now the UN headquarters for the region, and comes to a stop at the platform which terminates the new (Foundation) Promenade, with its view of old and new cities, the Mount of Olives and the mountains beyond the Dead Sea. Immediately below the promenade is a small Arab hamlet. The villagers complained that the massive earthmoving operations had changed the drainage patterns of the winter rain; the Foundation contractors put in new pipes. The Arab contractor accompanying Cheshin also points out that the new landscaping has wiped out the track which was the villagers' shortest access to the main road. Cheshin makes a note. The Foundation contractor is irritated by this new grievance; he maintains the villagers will profit from the promenade and that they submit too many complaints. Meanwhile, the village boys sell sesame rolls from a barrow on the still unfinished promenade, and below, in the valley, men carefully fence off their property with stones and sheets of iron.

A meeting between Kollek and Cheshin, some weeks later, to discuss current problems in the Arab districts shows the Mayor in two moods. There is Kollek the benevolent patron, and Kollek the troubled liberal.

As benevolent patron: bus trips are organized to the Galilee for Arab teachers in state schools, and the children are also taken on visits to archaeological sites and museums, the Jerusalem Foundation paying half the entrance fees. More problematic are the visits to municipal libraries in east Jerusalem, where children are charged a symbolic fee. The idea is not a success and this irritates Kollek: 'All right, so they won't read.' Cheshin tells Kollek some Arab families complain that they have to cart their rubbish to central collection points instead of having their own bins – a major problem in Jerusalem. Kollek replies: 'I saw a soldier in one of the new [Jewish] suburbs carrying his rubbish six hundred metres to the skip; so can they.' Cheshin informs Kollek that the Bet Sefafa villagers are still waiting for the Lands Authority to lower the price of land so that they can start on their new project. He makes a note; a few weeks later the matter is settled in their favour.

As troubled liberal: the Ibrahamiya school, with 1,300 pupils from kindergarten age to adolescence, has a two-year college faculty and wants to expand the school's development; a gym and swimming-pool complex are now under construction. The money comes from the Islamic Development Bank in Saudi Arabia and the school's maintenance is covered by tuition fees. All the school needs from the city is the permit to expand further. Kollek wants only to extend the kindergarten and elementary and high school facilities; not the college facility attended by five hundred students.

'We don't need a university in Jerusalem ... it'll become another Bir Zeit [the Palestinian university near Ramallah which is strongly nationalist and frequently closed down by the security forces].' Ironically enough, this was the very view expressed by Mubarak Awad.

Two months later, the local planning and building committee votes not to submit a plan for an addition to the school to the District Committee until the school's owners undertake to close its college wing. When this undertaking was given, the municipal council overruled the decision.

Cheshin reminds Kollek that *Al Fajr*, the east Jerusalem daily which publishes a weekly English edition distributed in the West Bank and abroad, spreads anti-Israel stories and makes trouble. Shouldn't it be closed? Kollek ponders. Does the Shin Bet (security force) have grounds for closing it? If not, he doesn't want to interfere.

On three issues – schools, the Palestinian press and housing – Kollek's efforts to encourage equality for the city's Arab population have met with obstacles which are fundamentally political; not so much open clashes between one national claim and another, but the problems involved in trying to act democratically towards a population which has no political rights.

By giving Arab parents the chance to opt for a Jordanian curriculum for their children, Kollek solved only part of the problem. The private schools, many of which are Christian institutions, are not under Israeli supervision and more than one of Kollek's advisors has voiced suspicions about what is taught there. Municipal inspectors have the right to visit the schools, but do not enforce it. Kollek would like to bring more children into the state system, but the budgets at his disposal do not allow him to improve the physical accommodation. Two hundred out of five hundred and forty Arab classes are housed in improvised quarters, some in rented rooms as much as a mile's walk from the main school buildings. Municipal officials wrestling with the problem find that Arab teachers will not use accommodation requisitioned from other Arabs – and the policy is not to defy them.

Another problem is the number of Arab children – no city official is prepared to venture an estimate – who have dropped out of classes before school-leaving age and work as pedlars, or in garages, work-shops and fields to help support their families. There are about 150 school dropouts in Jewish Jerusalem. Every motorist who drives regu-larly through the main crossroads between west and east Jerusalem, near the Damascus Gate, knows the 'tissue children', a pack of boys between eight and twelve who run between stationary cars at the traffic lights hawking boxes of Kleenex. But municipal inspectors are powerless: they can not check up on boys who say they go to private schools because they have no jurisdiction over them, and in any case they do not want to fine parents dependent on their children's labour. Once more 'allowing the Arabs to lead their own lives' means tolerating the open infringement of the law in the capital.

None the less, the city has done much to help the Arab children. It has introduced some fifty kindergartens – unknown previously in most Arab districts – special education classes for the handicapped, and buses to take deaf Arab children out to a western suburb for lessons. In deference to Arab custom, schools are not coeducational beyond kindergarten age. Last year, the city introduced advanced courses for teachers in Arab schools.

Kollek's views on the prospect of post secondary education in Jeru-salem indicate the limits of his liberalism in this respect. Another issue on which his record is ambivalent is that of the vigorously anti-Israeli press in east Jerusalem. Initially, Kollek was all for Arab self-expression in the capital. In November 1968, he guaranteed a $10,000 loan taken out by the publishers of *Al Kuds* (Jerusalem in Arabic), the leading daily, to restart their presses. Its editor, Mohammed Abu Zuluf, originally took a clearly pro-Jordanian line and on one occa-sion even asked for Israeli protection when one of his articles dis-pleased the PLO and his car was set on fire. But the line dividing the free expression of opinion and what the security forces see as incitement to rebellion has always been very thin indeed. The editors of Arab papers in the city have to apply for licences to the Ministry of the Interior, and the censorship rules by which they must abide are far more stringent than those which affect the Hebrew press.

After the appearance of *Al Kuds*, a number of extremely radical newspapers appeared in Jerusalem, *Al Fajr (The Dawn)* and *Al Shaab (The People)* among them, which competed for about ten thousand readers in Jerusalem and the West Bank. *Al Fajr*'s English language weekly is also an effective Palestinian propaganda sheet which highlights every instance of repression in the West Bank and every municipal problem concerning the Arabs in order to stress the hardships of life under occupation. In 1972 one of the editors of *Al Shaab* was deported and in August 1975 Kollek, the Minister of Police and the Attorney-General recommended that the paper should be closed down. Israeli journalists learned of the decision, and the protests inside Israel were so widespread that the idea was dropped.

There, in fact, was the core of the problem. Freedom of expression is indivisible, and it has repeatedly been argued that it is impossible to suppress Arab criticism of Israel's policies towards the Palestinians without also suppressing similar criticism in the Hebrew newspapers – which is often more effective, because better informed, than its Arabic equivalent. Moreover, Israeli and Palestinian journalists meet more frequently than any other professional group in the city; the Israelis are dependent on their Arab opposite numbers for information on east Jerusalem and West Bank affairs, while the Arabs know that many stories have a better chance of appearing in a Hebrew than in an Arab newspaper.

In the municipal context, Kollek has a particular problem with the Arab press. While his Arab Affairs Advisor keeps him in touch with the various published complaints about his administration, it is difficult for him to get a hearing in Arab newspapers. The editors of the more radical papers contact the municipality when they want a reaction, but rarely print the Mayor's letters. *Al Kuds* published Kollek's denial that municipal workers had violated Moslem tombs in the Mamilla cemetery in west Jerusalem (which the city is, in fact, now restoring after forty years of neglect); but it refused to take an article on municipal plans for Arab housing. The Interior Ministry openly favours papers like Esam El Anani's pro-Jordanian *An Nahar* (which recently published an interview with Kollek) over Hanna Siniora's *Al Fajr*, which was recently forbidden to distribute copies in the West Bank for a fortnight after publishing an interview with Yasser Arafat.

The decision to allow Palestinian newspapers to appear regularly in Jerusalem, to which Kollek was a party, was thus always problematic and has become even more so during the last couple of years, during which the intervention of the security authorities has again become obvious. Two smaller east Jerusalem newspapers were recently closed down on the grounds that they were financed by terrorist organizations and several reporters placed under 'town arrest' in the West Bank. Palestinian editors also argue that after the break between Jordan and the PLO, in February 1986, censorship became more stringent. Although since 1979 no Jerusalem Arab could be deported, the most recent editor of *Al Shaab*, Akram Haniye, who was resident in Ramallah, was ordered to be deported in November 1986 on the grounds that he was involved in terrorist activities on behalf of the PLO.

The Haniye case indicated very clearly how far the Arabs of Jerusalem had managed to enlist Israeli supporters on the issue of their civil rights. Haniye appealed to the Israeli Supreme Court. Israeli journalists, Knesset members and university teachers, among others, argued that if the security people had a case against Haniye, they should put him on trial. Public meetings organized together with Israelis were held at the Hakawati theatre in east Jerusalem – which exchanges visits with Israeli companies – and in Tel Aviv; Haniye's case was taken up in the Knesset by the Civil Rights Movement, and Israeli journalists who knew Haniye personally wrote impassioned defences of him; even the right-wing *Maariv* published articles suggesting that the real motives for Haniye's expulsion were political and not because he was a threat to national security. However, the case ended inconclusively. In January 1987, because the Supreme Court had refused to make the evidence against him available to his (Israeli) lawyers, Haniye abandoned the struggle and settled for deportation to Europe, thence to Algeria, a PLO stronghold, rather than to Jordan, where he was *persona non grata*.

Ultimately there is a basic contradiction in promoting a free press for people who are totally opposed to the regime which promotes it. Hence Kollek first encourages and then tries to curb the Palestinian press, and finally 'leaves it to the Shin Bet'.

Though Kollek and the city planners would like to keep the question of Arab housing apart from politics, this is impossible. Housing for the constantly growing Arab population is probably the most politicized issue in the city, because of what Israelis call 'the demographic problem'. What that means is that the Arab population of Jerusalem, which in 1967 was just over a quarter of the population, is now, according to official statistics, some 30 per cent; statisticians in the Ministry of Housing predict that by the year 2000 that number will have risen to 34 per cent. The proportion of Jews to Arabs has been kept relatively constant by Israel's building policies in the city, and the fact that until 1979 more Jews arrived in the capital than left it. That trend seems to have been reversed in the last few years: immigration is almost nil. The fertility rate for Jerusalem Arabs (like that of Oriental Israeli Jews) has dropped dramatically since 1967; according to a leading Hebrew University demographer, Arab women today bear less than half the number of children they did twenty years ago (Moslem women bearing 4.5 as against 9.7 children). Arab migration from the city to the surrounding Arab states has also contributed to narrowing the disparity between Arab and Jewish growth rates. Nevertheless, the Arab population continues to maintain a small lead, and Jerusalem, because of the work opportunities it offers, to attract Arabs from the West Bank.

The Ministry of Housing appears to believe that by not building homes for Arabs they will encourage their departure from the city. On the contrary, hundreds of homes have been built, either making use of the loophole in the planning laws or illegally, as extensions to existing buildings or even as separate units. But another solution has emerged which, though not openly discussed, has been accepted by all sides, for different reasons; this is large-scale building in villages and townships just outside the municipal limits, with municipal and government help. According to the officials involved, as many as 40,000 Arabs – of the official 120,000 – have moved outside the city into West Bank districts like A Ram, Azariya and Abu Dis within the last few years. A Ram, for instance, has grown from a few tens of houses in 1967 to a township housing about 20,000 people. The dimensions of such growth in east Jerusalem's Arab suburbs have been detected chiefly by the use of aerial photography.

Israel favours this solution because according to Israeli law the

Arabs are now living in Jordanian territory and no longer disturb the 'demographic balance'; the Arabs accept it for precisely the opposite reason – because for them the invisible frontier (unmarked on any road) does not exist. Here there is yet one more of Jerusalem's current anomalies: many Palestinians argue that the Arabs of the West Bank are better off than those in Jerusalem because they elect their own mayors, run their own municipal affairs, and so on. But in fact Jerusalem Arabs are very reluctant to forego a number of advantages they enjoy under Israel's direct rule, like national insurance payments (particularly advantageous for large families); participation in health benefits for those employed by Israelis; the right to work in Jerusalem, and the right to circulate freely in other parts of Israel. West Bank Arabs are not allowed to stay overnight in Israel without a special permit; they have special blue number plates on their cars which identify them and render them liable to searches and harassment by the police. This also exposes them, as will be seen, to reprisals by Jewish vigilantes.

Thus Israel has been obliged to allow those Arab families who agree to move out of Jerusalem to retain their Jerusalem identity cards. Recently, in January 1987, they were also permitted to remain eligible for national insurance payments. The only snag is that children born outside the city will not automatically enjoy these privileges.

As Jerusalem and the West Bank are in reality one economic unit, recognized as such by every government since 1967, the very growth of the city and its demand for unskilled labour has increased its attractiveness for the Arabs. So although some Israeli officials console themselves with the thought that Arabs are moving out of the city, it is beyond Israel's capacity, or desire, continually to search houses, separate families, or establish, within the city, who holds Jerusalem identity cards and who does not. Jerusalem and the West Bank are even closer in the economic and social sense under Israeli rule than they were before, because of the greater mobility of the population. Planners tacitly accept this in sketching the 'metropolitan area' of Jerusalem (which includes both the Jewish satellite towns in the West Bank and Arab villages) as one unit. But here the problem of the Jewish-Arab ratio returns once more, as the two populations in the 'metropolitan area' are exactly equal.

What this means for any future political settlement, time will tell.

The urgent problem, where the peace of Jerusalem is concerned, is the open wound at the centre of the city: the slum called the Moslem Quarter, where overcrowding exceeds anything known in Israel. In an area of less than a square kilometre, and where most of the buildings are more than a century old, live twenty-three thousand people (about the same number as in 1967), or about a fifth of the official estimate of the Arab population of the city. Statistics on this area have to be extracted from the general material on the city: in 1972 one-third of all Jerusalem Arab families were reported as living in one room, compared with 1 per cent of Jews. According to a recent survey, the number of Arab households with between three and four people to a room was three times that of the Jewish sector. The population density in the Moslem Quarter is twice as great as that in the old Jewish orthodox districts (the most overcrowded area in west Jerusalem), four times as great as that in the newer high density building districts, and ten times as great as that in the better-off Jewish and Arab residential areas elsewhere in the city.

Anyone who penetrates the courtyards and alleys behind the bazaars can see people living in conditions unimaginable elsewhere in Israel. There are cases of ten or twelve people to one room: parents with children who range from infants to adolescents. The 'water supply' may be no more than a rubber pipe leading from a tank on the roof of an outhouse to a sink in the courtyard, the 'kitchen' a cupboard. Winter heating, in ancient stone buildings, some medieval ruins, is often the same paraffin burner which is used to prepare the family's meals. According to the American woman who runs a Christian clinic in the Old City, there are families there who have to show their elder sons the door when there is nowhere for them to sleep.

During the period of mass immigration to Israel, in the 1950s, Jews lived in primitive conditions in the transit camps; and overcrowding was common in the early housing projects. But a vigorous social welfare and housing policy, as well as the later 'Project Renewal', a joint Israeli-Diaspora programme, has largely eliminated the Jewish slums. The Moslem Quarter is Jerusalem's chief problem today: drugs, theft, muggings are common. Many in the Christian community are moving out, beyond the walls; women are afraid to leave their homes after dark. This situation is virtually unknown to the Jewish public, and tourists, who rarely visit the Old City by night, and social welfare budgets have restricted the number of welfare workers. The violence in the Old City is turned against itself; people living there complain that the police do not crack down on notorious gangsters because these are the police informers, immune to arrest. Municipal officials warn that if something is not done soon, Kollek's proud assertion that Jerusalem is one of the world's safest cities will soon be disproved – at its very centre.

Kollek continually pleaded with successive Labour governments, during the 1970s, for the authority to 'thin out' the Moslem Quarter concurrently with the rehabilitation of the shrines and the bazaars. Despite the problems of resettling its residents in areas outside the city which still had no services, he argued that the difference between the rebuilt Jewish Quarter and the slums a few yards away was too glaring. But his efforts were complicated both by the government's response and by the refusal of many families to move. In 1976 he tried to persuade five hundred families to move to El Azariya, where land had been expropriated, mostly from the former Jordanian state (Arabs are always unwilling to settle on land taken from private Arab ownership). But the government had other ideas. They decided – perhaps in order to camouflage the turning over of Azariya to Arab tenants – to increase the area, by taking more private land, and simultaneously expropriating large tracts of land in Bet Jallah (near Bethlehem) and El Bireh (near Ramallah) for Israeli settlement. Many Arab families now refused to move from the Old City to Azariya.

Meanwhile, persuading Arabs to leave the Moslem Quarter became increasingly difficult. City officials who tried to negotiate sales found that the ownership situation was unbelievably complicated; buildings passed from one family to another and the actual owners were sometimes impossible to trace. Moreover, the inhabitants of the Moslem Quarter have become hostages to politics. They have been told by the PLO leadership that they are the guardians of the mosques on the Temple Mount; if they sell out to Jews, a death sentence is automatically pronounced on them by the Jordanian government. Nurses in a Christian clinic who try to teach birth control to women who at twenty-five already have seven or eight children are often told that the men insist on the women 'building a bridge' of children between Jerusalem and Amman. As soon as one family moves out of the Moslem Quarter, another, looking for rooms near the bread-winner's place of work, moves in. Buildings which are fit only for demolition are left to crumble because any initiative in the Old City is immediately condemned as an infringement of Arab rights.

In the 1980s, pressure on the Moslems of the Old City to remain as 'guardians of the mosques' was increased in the wake of Jewish terrorists' attacks on the Temple Mount. In April 1982, a recent American recruit to the Israeli army, Alan Goodman, shot his way past Arab guards and into the Dome of the Rock, whose walls were nicked by a hundred bullets from his machine-gun. Goodman killed two Moslems and injured eleven, in the worst incident on the Mount since the fire of 1969.

The government's reaction was slow and even-handed to the point of absurdity. Spokesmen deplored the damage to 'Holy Places sacred to Jews, Moslems and Christians', though there is no Christian shrine on the Temple Mount. Kollek compared the incident to recent assassination attempts on the lives of the Pope and President Reagan, and argued that there was no absolute defence against crazed attackers.

In March 1983, police uncovered a plan to storm the Mount by Jewish members of a weird cult who walk backwards and worship the sun; security was further tightened. But in January 1984, a far more serious attempt was made to lay explosives on the Mount, foiled by an alert Moslem guard who spotted the intruders. In the following April police apprehended a Jewish terrorist group which had been operating in the West Bank for nearly four years. Among their earlier crimes were murder and the attempted murder of three Palestinian mayors. Eighteen were put on trial for the attempt to blow up the Dome of the Rock, and these were not lunatics. They included leading members of the West Bank settlement community; all were observant Jews, most were farmers or professional men, and many had distinguished army records. Their attack on the Temple Mount, their hatred of the mosques, was related to messianic doctrines and the belief that the Mount had to be 'purified' of the Moslem presence before the Third Temple could be built.

Most of these men, who put their own definition of patriotism and their own interpretation of Jewish law above the laws of the country, have already been released from jail after serving only a part of their sentences. Hence the political pressures on the slum dwellers of the Old City not to abandon their place near the mosques has become even heavier.

It was during this period of counter-terror by Jewish extremists, on the Mount and in the Moslem Quarter, that the heads of the Christian communities considered joining the Moslem clergy in a formal complaint to the President of Israel, Chaim Herzog. A few days before Christmas 1983, the Greek Patriarch, Diodorus, approached Raphael Levy, the head of the District Planning Committee, and told him of a petition already signed by the Mufti, the head of the Supreme Moslem Council, and the Latin Patriarch, Mancini. The Armenian Patriarch, the Franciscan Custos and one leading member of the Greek Orthodox church were also considering supporting the Moslems, but the signature of the Greek Patriarch was obviously crucial. Together, Levy and Kollek persuaded Diodorus not to sign. No petition was presented.

The Moslem Quarter of the Old City has remained a problem not only in the political, but in the social sense for those who administer the city. For at its heart, behind the colourful stalls and the peaceful monastery courtyards – monasteries whose echoing corridors are paced by only a handful of priests – and behind the few tens of elegant houses belonging to the Palestinian élite, is the country's worst slum. Here, children can only grow up with bitter resentment against the rulers of the city. And it was here, last winter, that a murder took place that was to shake the city to its foundations. ·

6

The View from the Alleys

A T 3.40 ON A SATURDAY AFTERNOON last winter, 15 November 1986, a young man named Eliahu Amedi, identifiable as a Jew by his skullcap and beard, was walking along a quiet alley in the Old City when three young Arabs closed in on him. One held his arms from behind while the others whipped out kitchen knives and stabbed him. Amedi fought back desperately, broke free and managed to stumble a few yards into a main alley where he fell, with twelve knife wounds in his chest and stomach.

The killers ran uphill into the area of the markets, crowded with shoppers and tourists; one, who had been accidentally wounded by his fellows in the scuffle, was dragged along by the others. When they reached the enclosed courtyard of the Holy Sepulchre he collapsed on to a stone bench, and a few minutes later all three were caught. Passers-by who had seen them running had alerted the border police, special riot squads which regularly patrol the Old City.

Amedi lay where he had fallen, and within minutes a medical team was trying to revive him. But each of the twelve stab wounds was potentially fatal and he was already beyond help.

The incident was not the first of its kind in Jerusalem last year: there had been three previous stabbings. None was fatal, but not one of the assailants was caught. The Old City is a warren of alleys, with a thousand vaulted passages and winding lanes linked by steps where no wheeled vehicle can penetrate. 'Closing off the area', barring all entrances to the Old City, is not enough. Only those who know each house, each entrance – and each face – can hope to find attackers.

The aftermath is always the same. The iron shutters rattle down over the stalls in the alleys; their owners hurry home. Armed police stream into the Old City, dozens of young men are arrested, interrogated and released. Police encourage Israeli visitors in the Old City to go armed, in twos and threes. After a few days, the shops reopen, the tourists – unless they read the local papers – reappear. The Jewish response is indignant. Jews cannot walk safely in their own capital city, the police cannot keep order; extremists call for the death penalty for terror, or increased Jewish settlement in the Moslem Quarter.

Usually this is the end of the matter.

But not this time.

The first difference was that the killers were caught immediately – possibly because they were from out of town, from the West Bank town of Jenin. They had reached Jerusalem only that afternoon and picked their victim at random. He was the first young Jew whom they had managed to find alone, and they were out, as they later told the police, 'to kill a Jew' – any Jew. But had they deliberately set out to spread mayhem throughout the city, they could not have chosen their victim more skilfully.

For Eliahu Amedi belonged not just to one, but to two of the groups in the city among whom there were men who were bound to respond to the killing with violence and hysteria. Amedi was on his way to the Old City seminary he had recently joined, after a Sabbath spent with his family. The seminary was that of the Penitent Sons, the group which, intent on ousting their Arab neighbours from their homes, had caused so much trouble over the past few years. And Amedi's home district was Shmuel HaNavi, one of those working-class housing developments on the old frontier built in the 1950s for immigrants from Arab countries. The residents of Shmuel HaNavi had a number of grudges against government, city and police. Though recently included in an urban renewal project which had enlarged the cramped housing, they still had problems of unemployment and more than their share of delinquents. Sandwiched between the orthodox quarters of the city and the old frontier, with one of the luxurious new suburbs separated from it only by a main road connecting west and east Jerusalem, Shmuel HaNavi was the home of many young discontents, of whom some became religious 'penitents' and others joined the nationalist right wing. Amedi himself, by all accounts, was a gentle young man who had joined the seminary through religious conviction alone. The same could not be said of his mourners.

The trouble began during the night following the murder, on the site of the murder, near the seminary, and in the Shmuel HaNavi district.

The funeral procession, at the family's request, took place at dead of night and made its way from the seminary to the Mount of Olives cementary via the Damascus Gate. The family, friends and neighbours of Amedi were joined by hundreds of others, including supporters of the notorious Meir Kahana, the right-wing American rabbi who preaches racism and hatred of the Arabs. The procession staged a hysterical orgy of violence along the entire route they followed. They broke shop windows and the windscreens of parked cars; they burned a tractor parked in the main road and tried to set fire to the pumps of an Arab-owned petrol station. At one stage the bearers of the corpse, carried in a winding sheet according to the Jewish custom, on a stretcher, set the stretcher down and took part in the riot; as they passed the Basilica of the Agony at Gethsemane, they tried to break into the grounds. The police escort was forced to fire into the air several times as a warning.

Later that night, Molotov cocktails were thrown into the Arab shops and houses near the Penitent Sons' seminary. In the early morning of the next day, an Arab worker on his way from the Moslem Quarter to the Jewish Quarter was set on by a score of Jewish youths and beaten up; a Jewish bus driver, using his bus as a battering ram, smashed up cars and shop fronts in an Arab street. A young Arab student, one of a handful of east Jerusalem boys at the Hebrew University, was forced off a bus in north Jerusalem by an Israeli soldier and beaten up so badly that he needed treatment in hospital.

All the next day harassment of Arabs in the area near the seminary continued, and towards evening, in the Shmuel HaNavi quarter, hundreds of people spilled out on to the main road leading to east Jerusalem, which passed along the periphery of the district. These were, in the main, families who had come out of their houses looking for some kind of a focus of protest against the murder. They talked of the uselessness of the police, criticized the 'leftists' who sympathized with the Arabs, and complained of the burden of sharing the city. There were old gossips sitting on low garden walls, and mothers with young children and even babies. But there were also thugs with sackfuls of stones – the one weapon never in short supply in Jerusalem.

The police had been watching the district and soon a row of police jeeps was lined up on the further side of the road. Riot police, armed with tear gas canisters, plastic shields and night sticks, stood ready; but they clearly had orders neither to disperse the crowd nor to restrain them, but just to keep the main road open. The crowd suddenly came to life when reporters appeared and began taking pictures. The chanting began: 'Death to the Arabs', and the young men began scanning the passing traffic for cars with the blue number plates of the West Bank. As soon as one was spotted there was a scream of 'Arabs!' and a hail of stones flew, clattering against the sides of cars and lorries. Jewish cars were hit as well as Arab; one Arab driver was injured when a stone went through his windscreen. Each time this happened, the police made a token lunge at the crowd, which ran towards the buildings; mothers hid the smaller children's heads under their coats or dressing-gowns.

The scene was repeated night after night for most of the week that followed. The crowd, encouraged by the mild response, attacked the police, a press photographer and even a Knesset member, Ran Cohen of the Civil Rights Movement, who came to offer condolences to the bereaved family; he was set on by a group of young orthodox Jews and battered so violently that he needed nine stitches in his head.

Nothing like this had been seen in Jerusalem in the twenty years since the frontier was opened. There had been sporadic attempts to beat up Arabs after the worst terrorist outrages, but the police had quickly checked and contained them. Stone throwing, until now, had been the Arabs' chief protest on the streets against the Israeli presence. After each of the attacks on the Temple Mount the Arabs had gathered, throwing stones and chanting 'Death to the Jews'. From refugee camps on the borders of Jerusalem stones were often thrown at Jewish cars and buses, and passengers were wounded. Police and army pursued the offenders and punished them severely.

Now it was the Jews' turn. Much of the violence was clearly organized – in the Old City to terrorize the seminarists' neighbours; in Shmuel HaNavi to frighten away Arabs. A cobbler's shop near the seminary, whose owner had been urged by the Sons to sell out, was gutted by fire. A nearby grocery shop was broken into by men described as 'in orthodox dress'. The family living in the courtyard below the seminary were pelted by stones and fled the city to Hebron. All this despite what the police described as 'a stepped-up police presence'.

In 1968, after far more serious terrorist attacks in which tens were killed or wounded, the government had spoken out immediately against reprisals, and had done so effectively. Now during the first twenty-four hours the only leader to speak out was Teddy Kollek.

His first response was typically blunt and furious. He condemned the murder but said that he was even more shocked by the rioting. Such behaviour, he added, amounted to co-operation with the PLO, which wanted to prove that Jews and Arabs could not live together in the city.

This was exactly, almost word for word, what Moshe Dayan had told Jewish rioters after an Arab bomb outrage in 1968. But this time, the rebuke was received with fury. The crowds in Shmuel HaNavi shouted 'Teddy's an Arab' and even 'Death to Teddy' as well as 'Nazi police'. Advised that a visit to the district would be dangerous, the Mayor stayed away. A twenty-four-hour police watch was put outside Kollek's flat in the Rehavia district of west Jerusalem.

There was still no vigorous action by the government. Prime Minister Shamir, almost a day later than Kollek, echoed his sentiments, but the Minister of Police, the (Labour) Haim Bar Lev, who was abroad, saw no urgent reason to return to Israel.

Again ahead of anyone in the government, Kollek visited the Old City. But this time his strictures were cautious; he told television reporters that the seminarists were 'nuisances' and that, after things calmed down, the subject of their presence in the Moslem Quarter would have to be reviewed. Meanwhile, Kollek summoned the head of the Arab Chamber of Commerce, Fayek Barakat, and a score of merchants and *mukhtars* to City Hall and invited a television team. Lights were set up in the Council Room; but the Arabs objected, insisting that the team remove itself. Kollek was obliged to be interviewed outside in the hall, where he explained that he was about to tell the Arabs that they must restrain the extremists in their midst.

The merchants and *mukhtars* now entered the Council Chamber. There were respectable-looking citizens in three-piece suits and dark glasses, and the *mukhtars* with their headcloths and worry beads. There were no smiles or preliminary courtesies. The Mayor spoke Hebrew, the merchants Arabic or English. They listened, impassive, to Kollek's tirade – part rebuke, part warning – about the passivity of Jerusalem Arabs while their young men terrorized the city. He reminded them of what he had done for all the residents. Had he not persuaded the police and the army, time and again, not to open shops by force when the merchants closed them in political protest? Had he not tried to preserve normality in the city and encourage the tourist trade which was their living? For this reason he had objected to a heavy police presence in the Old City.

But the merchants had to understand, said Kollek, that the police could not keep order alone; they needed co-operation from the local people. 'I don't expect you to make a political declaration,' said Kollek, glancing round the table, 'but [and here he mimicked an Old City merchant sitting in his stall] don't raise your eyes to heaven and say that "nothing can be done". In your schools, in your cafés, pass on the message!'

One of the shopkeepers, who said that he had heard of the murder only that morning in church, asked how on earth he could be held responsible for murderers who came from outside the city?

Kollek flapped his hand irritably. 'I wouldn't have called this meeting had this been a terrorist action,' he said. 'I didn't call you in after the incident at the Dung Gate. These are young people with knives, their motive is individual hatred. It's a question of the education of young people; society can influence them.'

The merchants appeared quite unmoved. They clearly regarded the summons to the Council Chamber as the chance to put their own point of view. One pointed out that Arabs and Jews were not treated equally in such cases; when Arabs committed a murder, their houses were destroyed. When Alan Goodman (the Jew who had killed Arabs on the Temple Mount) did so, nothing had happened to his family. There was also the question of the Mamilla cemetery, where Moslem bones had been dug up when the city built a parking lot ... Kollek scarcely waited to hear the translation; the word Mamilla was enough. He pointed out that he himself had opposed the destruction of terrorists' houses in Jerusalem, with the result that they had been left standing, which was, he said, 'a great achievement'. As for Mamilla, the ex-Mufti, Haj Amin el Husseini, had built a hotel on a Moslem cemetery in mandatory times; the bones in question had been accidentally disturbed and buried with all ceremony. Kollek paused for a moment.

'I don't say it's an ideal situation. I wouldn't want to be an Arab in Jerusalem.' Then suddenly his temper snapped. 'Where will all these complaints get you? All I ask of you is to try and keep the peace. Don't bring your complaints to me now. This isn't a debating society!'

But the merchants stood their ground. They complained that people were continually being stopped by police or soldiers. They complained of car searches. 'Tell me the numbers of the soldiers and the cars,' said Kollek. 'I'll see it doesn't happen again.'

'This is a difficult time,' Kollek concluded. 'We are open to all suggestions.' Then he invited them to submit other complaints, and several took him at his word. The meeting which had begun with Kollek's impassioned appeal to the merchants to stop the murders, ended with the request that he mend the leaking sewage outlet at the Damascus Gate.

Later, Fayek Barakat said: 'It was a very useful opportunity for us to bring up a few things that had been bothering us.'

The week wore on. Several terrorized Arab families who lived in the alley near the seminary left their homes and took shelter with relations, or camped out in the Cotton Market a few yards away, where they felt safer. Hearing rumours that the Penitent Sons had stashed weapons in the seminary, the police searched the premises, but, perhaps predictably given the military experience of some of the seminarists, found nothing. The police were in fact no match for the Sons; on a couple of occasions, they gave an alarm in one alley and, while the police rushed there, attacked another building.

During the week, Amir Cheshin, Kollek's Advisor on Arab Affairs, tried to make peace between the seminarists in the Moslem Quarter (excluding the Penitent Sons) and the Arab residents, in a formal *sulha*, the Moslem ceremony of reconciliation. While the impenitent Sons brooded behind closed doors and windows and the police stood watch outside, Cheshin held his *sulha* on neutral ground, the surgery of a Jewish woman dentist who for some time had practised in the Moslem Quarter.

But despite the surface courtesy, resentment emerged on both sides. The Arabs reminded the Jews that none of their complaints against the Penitent Sons had been effective, the Jews retaliated by asking what the Arabs would do to protect Jews from further knifings. One Jew claimed that he had himself put out a fire in an Arab house; and agreed that there was nothing a civilian could do against armed attackers. The Arabs claimed that no one had witnessed the attack on Amedi – something borne out by the chief of the Jerusalem police, Tat Nitzav Yehudai, who told the municipal Council, in a closed briefing, that the murder had taken place not outside the seminary, as published, but in a side alley and that 'it was hard to blame the residents' for what had happened.

Cheshin was in a difficult situation; though clearly indignant at the inadequate police protection for the Arabs, it was hard for him to publicly take their part against the police. The press, meanwhile, fully alerted to the *sulha*, was waiting outside to broadcast the success of Kollek's initiative. But so were other bystanders, with other ideas.

When Cheshin emerged and began to read out the statement that a joint neighbourhood team would henceforth meet to prevent friction between Jews and Arabs, another Jewish 'penitent' settler from the Moslem Quarter, notorious for his hostility to Arabs, screamed, 'No pardon! No atonement! Out with the Arabs!'. Further up the alley, a group of Arab women began to wave their fists and shout, 'Palestine! Palestine!' The cameras duly recorded the scene, and within hours the stone throwing and arson had recommenced. Those who had agreed to the *sulha* were not those who had started the trouble.

The police and the politicians tried to play down the incidents, even as they were happening. They insisted that the riots in Shmuel HaNavi were the work of a few 'provocateurs' – Kahana's bully boys and the 'familiar faces' from the police files – and that the crowds who appeared nightly were dragged in against their will. Unfortunately, this version was contradicted by the head of the Shmuel HaNavi neighbourhood committee, Avi Elsam, who was also a member of Kollek's own municipal faction. While municipal officials tried to clear the district's name, and Jewish community leaders in Washington who had contributed to the urban renewal plan sent messages of continuing support, Elsam insisted that the nightly demonstrations were a sign of 'community involvement' and that it was a very good thing that the death of one of the community was so deeply felt by all. He said that all the neighbourhood had been on the street and backed their right to demand that 'no Arab should enter our district' (to which Kollek retorted: 'Then who will clean your streets?'). So far from attempting to calm tempers, Elsam promised more trouble at the end of the mourning period.

During all this time there was little reaction from the government. The presence of the seminaries in the Moslem Quarter had become a political issue, supported by the governing right wing and the religious parties, who refused to disown any 'penitents' whatever their actions. Politics was inevitably reflected in the special meeting of the City Council called to discuss the murder and the riots.

Only Kollek's faction, One Jerusalem, was outspoken in its condemnation of both the murder and the rioters. Everyone knew the Penitent Sons were gangsters, said Kollek's Deputy Mayor, Avraham Kehilla; Emmanuel Sussman, the main Labour man in the faction, was indignant over Elsam's speeches: 'Who gave him the right to speak for the whole community?'

But Rabbi Meir Porush, head of the Agudat Israel faction, wanted only to discuss the murder. He suggested that there should be radical changes in Israel's policy towards the Jerusalem Arabs. 'If the Arabs don't co-operate with the authorities,' he said, 'they've got to be frightened into it.' He accused Kollek of failing to encourage Jewish settlement in the Old City and resented the Mayor's definition of the Penitent Sons as 'nuisances'. 'Are you calling Eliahu Amedi, may his memory be blessed, a nuisance?' Kollek was forced to admit that the term was perhaps unfortunate. A Herut councillor suggested that the entire Moslem Quarter be handed over to the company which had reconstructed the Jewish Quarter. Deputy Mayor, Nissim Ze'ev, of the Sephardi Torah Guardians' party, implicitly defended the stoning of the left wing Knesset member who had visited the Amedi family, arguing that his visit had been 'a provocation'. It was only after much argument that Kollek succeeded in moving a resolution condemning the murder, the rioters and 'the blackening of the name of the Shmuel HaNavi district'.

During that week of hatred and fear, there was another important funeral. Anwar Nusseibeh, the most respected Palestinian figure in the city, died of cancer. Kollek visited him in hospital days before his death. He subsequently said that Nusseibeh had told him that 'had he been Governor of Jerusalem' he would have ordered the killers of Amedi hanged. When they were put on trial a few weeks later, the three young men said that they felt no remorse. 'In any case,' said one confidently, 'we're bound to be freed at the next exchange of prisoners.'

Nusseibeh's funeral was organized by Feisal el Husseini of the Supreme Moslem Council; the procession of hundreds of men left

the Nusseibeh house, just off the main Nablus Road, passed the Anglican cathedral with its spire and courtyard so reminiscent of the
country where Nusseibeh had studied, down the busy street where
passers-by stood silent and through the Damascus Gate. It passed
through the alleys descending through the markets and, by the Cotton
Gate, into the precincts of the Temple Mount to the Al Aqsa mosque.

First came a contingent of little boy scouts in green uniforms, musicians with recorders and bagpipes, then mourners carrying the huge
velvet green and red ceremonial flags of the Wakf, and tall, waving
palm fronds, the Moslem symbol of mourning; the music played
was an adaptation of European marches. At the Mount, the Moslem
clergy gathered to receive the procession, which could be heard from
some distance, as the hundreds of young men walking behind the
plain pine coffin shouted, in time to their step: 'In fire, in blood,
we shall redeem you, O Palestine.' As they entered the precincts,
the shouts, in English for the journalists, became briefer: 'Israel No!
P-L-O!'

Policemen stationed at the gates called urgently into their walkie-
talkies, Moslem guards gestured away groups of tourists, including
a chattering, merry crowd of Philippine Christians posing behind
a bright yellow tour advertisement on the steps of the Dome of the
Rock. The cortège made its way across the great space between the
Dome and the Al Aqsa, and the coffin was borne into the mosque
accompanied by Nusseibeh's sons and the clergy. One rather embar-
rassed looking figure detached himself from the cortège and made
for the Moors Gate: Shlomo Toussia-Cohen, the Electricity Corporation's Israeli lawyer, once Kollek's right-wing rival for the post
of mayor.

While the crowd waited silently for the coffin to emerge, only a
few yards away, at the Western Wall below the Mount, a Tunisian
Jewish family was celebrating the bar mitzvah of one of their sons;
they had arrived at the Wall just as the muezzin ended his mourning
chant, which carried right across the Wall plaza. Now the boy was
carried up to the Wall on his father's shoulders, greeted by women
ululating shrilly, fingers quivering in their mouths, while his male
relations played a welcoming fanfare on drums and cymbals. Above,
Nusseibeh's body was borne away to the Moslem cemetery to the
east of the Mount; at the Wall, the young Jew read his portion of

the Scrolls of the Law, and assumed the responsibilities of manhood.

On the steps leading from the Wall plaza to the Old City markets, a poster announced a mass demonstration to be held outside the seminary, on the eighth day after the murder, the end of the first Jewish mourning period. On this day it is customary for the family to visit the grave, but on that afternoon there was also another procession: the Penitent Sons, Kahana's thugs and a few tens of Amedi's neighbours again led a rampage through the alleys. The Arabs closed their shops, shuttered their windows and remained indoors, as the young men kicked at doors, broke any visible window and roughed up one young Arab who got in their way. The police, they later explained, had allowed the demonstration to take place because it was 'a religious procession'.

After this, the violence ran dry. The Arabs had put up no resistance save for a few stones flung at police cars. The reporters had wrung the most out of the week's events with headlines like 'Jerusalem explodes' and 'Funeral candles and Molotov cocktails'. It was agreed that this was nothing compared with Beirut and Belfast; apart from Amedi, no one was dead. No one who had not driven or walked through the Shmuel HaNavi quarter, or the Haldiyeh alley, that week, before the stones were shovelled off the road and the heaps of charred rags and furniture were carted out of the alley, would have known that anything untoward had happened in the city. In Jerusalem, what happens deep in the alleys is inaudible from the city outside the walls.

Kollek came to an agreement with the government that it would reimburse the city's expenses if they repaired the damage to the homes and shops in the Moslem Quarter. After everything was over, the Minister in charge of Arab Affairs, Moshe Arens, visited the Old City with an enormous escort of border police and soldiers – young recruits who had been called into Jerusalem that week for the first time in years. Kollek met Arens at the Damascus Gate but refused to walk through the Old City with the Minister. 'I don't intend to walk in Jerusalem with any army escort,' Kollek protested angrily, and followed on alone.

That the violence could have been swiftly contained was made clear only two months later. Two brothers shopping in the Old City were stabbed in the back in the market only yards from the site of the Amedi murder; the attackers escaped. The victims were from the Musrara district, an area no less hostile to the city's Arabs than Shmuel HaNavi, and for similar reasons. But this time the police moved in fast to cordon off the entire district, and Victor Suissa, the local neighbourhood leader, urged restraint. When Kollek visited the wounded in hospital he was not well received by the victims' families, who told him that instead of reading the riot act to the Jews he should make the streets safe from Arabs. 'I understand the anger, but if we give in to it, this city will become a second Beirut,' Kollek was quoted as saying. What the papers did not report, however, was that the same evening, Kollek, ending his day's work with a visit to an all-night café near the Musrara district, overheard a group of youths talking about the stabbings. 'The city does nothing, the police do nothing, the government does nothing,' they told the Mayor angrily. "We're going in there tomorrow to take the Old City apart.'

Kollek invited them to come to his office the following morning to talk it over. There he sat with them for nearly four hours, arguing with fifty boys about Jews, Arabs and Jerusalem. He managed to give them the impression that the fate of the city rested in their hands, that they would be responsible for what happened next. They did not 'take the Old City apart', though Kollek was not sure how long the effects of his talk would last. 'But,' he asked, 'supposing I hadn't gone into that café that night?'

That question was important above all for Teddy Kollek himself. For the revival of terror and counter violence in the city had given the Mayor back the sense of how important his contribution was to the city, how he had stood up in public almost alone among Israel's official leadership, for reason and moderation after the Amedi murder. It revived his reputation which, for many months now, had been under a cloud. People now recalled that Kollek had tried to remove the Penitent Sons' seminary from the Moslem Quarter, but had been defeated by orthodox and right-wing political interests, with no help from his Labour colleagues; that Kollek had reminded Israel, time and again, that 'the roots of tolerance in the city are very shallow', and that the neglect of Arab interests was producing a new generation in which political frustration was intensified by social deprivation.

Abroad, the riots in Jerusalem were seen as a setback to Kollek's policies in the city. Soon after the Amedi murder and its sequel, Kollek received a private telegram of support from Chancellor Helmut Kohl of West Germany. It was significant that Kollek's first reaction was to assume that the telegram referred not to the bloodshed in Jerusalem, but to his own ordeal at the hands of the Israeli media, which had reached its climax during the week immediately preceding the Amedi murder. In fact, at the time of the murder he had been on the point of resigning as Mayor of Jerusalem.

Kollek's ordeal had begun just a year earlier, with the arrest of Mordechai Darwish, the head of the Municipality's Urban Improvement Department. Other municipal officials were subsequently named in one of the longest investigations ever carried out in the capital by the local police fraud squads. They were not to be finally indicted until December 1986, when Darwish faced charges on 125 counts of theft and bribery, while other officials were involved in charges of fraud and breach of trust, including stealing from the pension fund of which Darwish was chairman.

Mordechai Darwish had been one of the better-known employees in Kollek's city administration; a municipal official for thirty-one years, he had been Jerusalem's chief gardener during the time that Kollek had painted the city green. But the problem was not that Kollek was in any way involved in Darwish's alleged misdoings.

Very early in the investigation, the police decided to reveal the existence of a private discretionary bank account in the Mayor's name, from then on called the 'Teddy Fund', money given to him by friends abroad to distribute for the city's benefit as he saw fit. Those who had received allocations from this fund, for purposes such as buying cars, taking study trips in Israel and abroad, and to ease their financial situation in general, were a great number of municipal officials, members of Kollek's faction, and even Raphael Levy, the head of the District Planning Committee, who had accompanied the municipal representatives to London to study the 'borough' scheme.

A police file was opened on Kollek and for several months the enquiry dragged on. Kollek and his beneficiaries were interrogated by the police and eventually the file was passed to the Attorney-General, Yosef Harish. In September 1986, Harish announced he had not found that Kollek had committed any crime in establishing and maintaining the fund, or used the fund in bad faith — that is, as the police had suggested during their investigation, to bribe public officials. Nevertheless, Harish added that the fund 'conceals a danger that in certain circumstances it might be used in contravention of proper administrative procedures'.

Kollek, in administering a private system of incentives and rewards, had not broken the law; but he had bypassed the system. Municipal budgets and salaries were inadequate and did not provide much leeway for experimentation and innovation.

While awaiting the verdict of the Attorney-General, Kollek, who had handed over all the relevant documents to the police — but was unable, in several cases, to remember exactly where the money had gone — announced, with unusual humility, that should the Fund be declared illegal he would suspend its operation. The Fund was not suspended.

When the final decision was announced at a meeting of the City Council, all the members drank a toast to the Mayor. The leader of the Likud opposition, Reuven Rivlin, said that 'what Teddy suffered during the investigation would have broken a lesser man', and Kollek thanked the opposition for not exploiting the investigation for political gain. All was sweetness and light. But Kollek's relief was to be short-lived.

On 9 November, Raphael Levy was arrested together with an unnamed east Jerusalem cleric, later revealed as Shahe Ajamian, the wealthy, worldly Armenian archbishop whom Kollek and Levy had attempted — unsuccessfully — to have reinstated by the Patriarch five years previously. Levy was later charged with misuse of public office, bribe-taking and various currency offences. Ajamian was held in police detention for over a month and then released on heavy bail. He was not formally charged, though police sources quoted by the reputable Hebrew press said that he was suspected of bribery, smuggling and the unauthorized possession of firearms. Though the rare previous arrests of clergymen — on security offences — had been vigorously opposed by all the local churches, their silence over the Ajamian case was deafening. Later, it was reported that an unnamed archbishop (from another church) was to be given immunity in exchange for providing evidence for the prosecution of Levy. When these arrests took place, Kollek was in Holland, raising money for a park to be laid out in the southern part of the city and including a windmill, canals, a Dutch coffee shop, an 'Amsterdam corner' and a lake complete with swans. He emerged from an audience with Queen Beatrix straight into the arms of reporters who asked him to react on reports that, on his return to Israel, he was again to be interrogated by the police.

Kollek was not, in fact, under suspicion, and when he was subsequently questioned on his professional relations with Levy (who, as head of the District Planning Committee, was obviously a close colleague), it was not under oath. Nevertheless, it took four days for Kollek's loyal and perpetually harassed Hebrew press spokesman, Rafi Devara, to prod the police into issuing a clear statement to this effect. During this period – and after it – the police, the press and even some of Kollek's former colleagues continued to chip away at the Mayor's reputation.

There was no denying that Kollek's legendary ambition to get things done fast had made him impatient with administrative and bureaucratic delays. Nor could it be denied that Levy had consistently endorsed most of the projects put to him by Kollek's local planning office, perhaps not the role that should have been played by an independent public servant. The press recalled that Levy had proposed an amendment to the District Planning Law to the effect that building in the Old City should not be open to public inspection – an amendment all too clearly framed to speed plans for the reconstruction of the Greek Orthodox patriarchate, which had been so forthcoming in leasing land to the city. This proposal had been sharply criticized by the then Deputy Attorney-General, Yoram Bar Sela, who had reprimanded Levy for allowing builders to exceed their formal limitations on other occasions. The press also brought up the matter of the half-finished Armenian Cathedral on Mount Zion, begun in the mid 1970s under Ajamian's aegis, which – though condemned as preposterous in scale by all city and district planners – had nevertheless been pushed through by Kollek and Levy. The papers reminded their readers that Levy had backed the renovation of the old football stadium in a residential district on absurd 'environmental' grounds, because this was Kollek's wish; and stated that Kollek's was the 'broad back', as they put it, on which Levy had relied in his various interventions in church politics. It was not denied that Kollek had tried to secure the release of Ajamian – not officially charged with any crime – on bail, and the fact that the wily Armenian 'had done the state some service' (unspecified tasks for Israel which could not be revealed) was not particularly helpful to Kollek. To make matters even worse, Levy's lawyer, Shlomo Toussia-Cohen, was caught smuggling a letter addressed to Kollek out of jail with Levy's dirty linen. The letter allegedly threatened the Mayor that if he did not intervene with the Prime Minister and government for his release, Levy would 'not remain silent'. Israel's libel laws are rarely implemented and the press circumspect only on security affairs, and one barb after another of this kind was launched at the hapless Mayor, without it even being specified what, precisely, he himself was supposed to have done.

All Kollek's enemies – former rivals, Labour Party officials who envied him his successes, the environmentalists whom he had so often, and so contemptuously, dismissed – began to talk about the end of Kollek's career and the hubris which had now overtaken him. Every crisis in Israel has a pseudo-biblical equivalent in conversation, and people quoted the verse from Proverbs: 'If a ruler hearken unto lies, all his servants are wicked.' The Knesset Finance Committee held up a grant of some ten million dollars promised to the municipality on the grounds, rumour had it, that municipal affairs were not being properly conducted. Kollek appeared on television and for the first time in his career appeared humbled, vulnerable. He complained that the constant attacks on his reputation were making it impossible for him to work, and that he no longer felt that he was of service to the city, that the attacks were endangering his credibility with the benefactors who had supported the Foundation, and that he was considering his resignation.

New candidates sprang up overnight for the Mayor's job – from right across the political spectrum, and including not only the standing rival, Rivlin, but a film actor turned religious penitent, Uri Zohar. There was consternation amongst Kollek's followers. In the municipality, work slowed to a standstill at the administrative level, as heads of departments hesitated to present plans for the Mayor's approval. There were frantic consultations among his faction and in the local Labour Party branch. Kollek was urged to remain for the sake of the city, for the sake of peace and coexistence between Jews and

Arabs, for the sake of those who had supported him faithfully at five elections. Concerned citizens took out full-page ads in the newspapers to express their solidarity with the Mayor. Campaign stickers from the 1983 municipal elections, 'I'm for Teddy', were unearthed and redistributed. Volunteer workers who had helped Kollek run welfare projects planned to plant a grove of pine trees in the Mayor's name (in plastic bags, of course, because of the sabbatical year).

It was in the midst of this domestic uproar, on a November afternoon, that Eliahu Amedi, on his way back from a Sabbath with his family, was set upon and murdered.

The period between the arrest of Raphael Levy and the final explosion of anger by Jewish hooligans in the Moslem Quarter covered no more than two weeks. But during this period, two things became clear to those concerned with the future of Israeli rule in Jerusalem. One was the fragility of all those delicate accommodations which maintained the peace of the city. The other was the realization, delayed for so long but now faced for the first time by Kollek's supporters, of how much depended on one man's image, style and abilities.

If what had happened in the city justified Kollek's warnings, however, it also indicated that without firm backing by the govenment even he could not control a mob which had gotten out of hand. Kollek had not volunteered to mount a soapbox in Shmuel HaNavi, and, even had he done so, it is unlikely that he would have been treated differently from Ran Cohen, the left-wing Knesset member who came to offer condolences and left to have his head stitched in hospital.

The events of November had restored to Kollek his sense of importance, the confidence that Jerusalem needed him. But the shock to his supporters in the city was more profound. Even those who had been most critical of Kollek began to wonder about the alternative. What had happened to Kollek in Jerusalem had had a parallel in national politics in 1977, the year of the great swing to the right after thirty years of Labour domination. Labour had been too long in power and was over-confident; there were persistent rumours of corruption in the lower administrative orders; the intellectuals had become disenchanted with Labour, and their fragmentation, in political terms, had invited a right-wing victory. But what was, in fact, the alternative to Kollek's policies?

Reuven Rivlin, front runner for the right-wing Likud, has never challenged Kollek openly for the post of mayor. He praises Kollek as the man who has made Jerusalem into an international landmark. But, he adds, Kollek has recently gone too far beyond the administrative limitations of his office as mayor, has begun to assume the prerogatives of a ruler. Above all, Rivlin asserts, Kollek has forgotten that his ability to rule Jerusalem is dependent on Jewish sovereignty, has gone out of his way to show a liberal spirit towards the Arabs, and has earned the enmity of the ultra-orthodox.

What, then, would Rivlin do that Kollek has failed to do? Firstly, says Rivlin, the Likud would devote far more time to the actual running of the city and less to its foreign relations. While the Likud is all for equal services for every resident of the city, help to the Arabs would be dependent on their agreement to be part of Jewish Jerusalem.

What does that mean? The Arabs' right to housing, says Rivlin, would depend not only on the payment of municipal taxes, but on their performing some kind of 'national service' which would prove their loyalty to Israel.

What about housing for the Arabs? Rivlin says that there is no lack of Arab housing, but that much of it is illegal. All illegal building, he says sharply, would be destroyed 'on the spot'; those who needed accommodation would be moved 'with government co-ordination' outside the municipal limits of the city.

As for the slums of the Moslem Quarter, they would be cleaned up, thinned out and given the same treatment as the Jewish Quarter. It could not be expected that a slum clearance project would be carried out by Israel for the Arabs' benefit. The aim would be to resettle Jews in as much of the Old City as possible. 'If the Arabs haven't made any improvements in the Old City for two thousand years, the Jews aren't going to do it for them.'

There could be no political immunity for the Moslem Quarter. 'The Moslem Quarter isn't as sensitive as the mosques [on the Temple Mount]. We'd leave that alone. We can't possibly rebuild on the Temple Mount.' Rivlin says that he would – again with government co-operation – remove the offending Penitent Sons' seminary from the Moslem Quarter. 'If I had an Arab maid, I wouldn't allow Jews to behave to her as they behaved to the Arabs in their neighbourhood.'

But the presence of the other, well behaved seminaries in the Moslem Quarter was 'a positive thing'.

The Wakf, of course, would protest against this policy. 'Zionists have been fighting for a hundred years against protests. We have to be resolute.'

Rivlin argues that the Likud would govern Jerusalem more efficiently than Kollek, who threw the Agudat Israel orthodox out of his coalition when he no longer needed them; the Likud would be prepared to form a coalition with the orthodox, on condition that this did not harm the freedom of the secular Jewish majority in the city.

He does not think that fund-raising for Jerusalem would suffer from Kollek's departure: 'People give to Jerusalem, not just to Teddy Kollek.' There might be a refusal by some donors to give to a Jerusalem ruled by the Likud. But in any case, the future of the Foundation would be reviewed. The point was that Kollek's successor would have entirely different priorities. A Likud mayor, with the help of a right-wing government – and Rivlin is consistently emphatic that none of the new measures could be carried out without government help – would act to eliminate the anomalies regarding the Arabs of Jerusalem, and aim for a Jerusalem with a much stronger Jewish majority.

One Jerusalem, Kollek's faction, was created in its maker's image. Kollek's campaigns have changed over the years. His first election campaign was run as a maverick, with a young and energetic team, during a period of political stagnation. When Kollek rejoined the Labour Party, in 1969, he was able to call on the Jerusalem Labour Party machine, which worked quietly and efficiently in the 'neighbourhoods' – the working-class districts – while Jerusalem's smart set – the businessmen and the contractors, the university lecturers and the other Jerusalem intellectuals – lobbied among their colleagues and raised money both in Israel and among Kollek's supporters abroad. According to Kollek's campaign managers of that time, the two groups never met, functioned among different sectors of the electorate, and so managed to defeat the Likud machine which kept Jerusalem solidly a right-wing city at the national elections.

But by the time Kollek had established his One Jerusalem list for the elections of 1978, the entire structure had come to depend on his prestige and personality. The question in early 1987 was: could it survive without him?

Kollek has often been criticized, in the past, for not having 'named a successor' — a naive enough complaint, for men like Teddy Kollek do not appoint heirs. His own reaction to the question is: 'Did Churchill appoint a successor?' But there is more in question than the identity of Kollek's successor: can the policies he has established survive his departure?

Meeting at the house of one of Kollek's most solid supporters in mid December 1986 was a deeply worried group of men and women: veteran Labour and municipal officials, businessmen and contractors, and a couple of concerned outsiders. The consensus was that the faction had no staff, no money, and no clear programme with which to go to the voters in two years' time. The all-important question was: would Kollek run, or wouldn't he? They feared for the future of Jerusalem should it 'fall into the hands of Ruby Rivlin or Uri Zohar'. Many of those present felt that they had not risen effectively to Kollek's defence during his ordeal. But there were two views on whether this would have been useful. Did Kollek need their help — a man who had never needed anyone's help before; would it not, rather, have been an admission of weakness to accept it, had it been offered?

The second question was whether funds could be raised for a campaign with any other candidate. One leading Jerusalem industrialist said that he had been offered an immediate donation, by a foreign benefactor, of $50,000 on condition that he would guarantee that Kollek was the candidate at the next municipal elections. He had been obliged to refuse the offer. Kollek had, after all, threatened to resign; he was seventy-five years old; if he ran again, he would be over eighty by the end of his term of office. One of Kollek's ex-aides suggested that they should all ask Kollek, outright, for an answer, so that they could find another candidate if necessary. A Labour man said: 'If you ask Teddy today if he'll run, he'll answer no, because that's how he feels today; then we'll have no Teddy, and no money either.'

Several of Kollek's veteran supporters were clearly exasperated by his refusal either to confirm that he was running, or to name a possible successor. Labour men insisted that any future candidate could not be a man identified with the Labour Party. He would have to be someone 'above politics', but 'in the national league'.

Here a young outsider quietly offered his views. He said that there were wide groups of potential supporters in the city that One Jerusalem had not canvassed. 'I don't know whether any of you have noticed,' he said, 'but I wear a skullcap. I hope that doesn't put me beyond the pale.' The officials hastened to reassure him. He made three proposals: the faction needed more 'momentum' even in mid term. One Jerusalem should begin to formulate Kollek's policy, but without Kollek himself. All previous campaigns, and their slogans, had stressed the man: 'Give Teddy a hand', 'I'm for Teddy', and so on. But with all due respect, the man was clearly nearing the end of his career. Thirdly, he thought the party should go on to the offensive and point out the alternative to Kollek. 'You've got to frighten people,' he said, 'you've got to show them what can happen here' – and he quoted the latest survey showing that young, well-educated people were leaving the city, abandoning it to the ultra-orthodox and the Arabs.

The contractor who had canvassed funds abroad agreed: 'People are talking quite openly about leaving the city,' he said. 'They're giving up.'

In Arab Jerusalem, too, apprehension was growing. At a meeting between Jews and Arabs called by Kollek's supporters, several Arabs warned of disquieting developments in east Jerusalem. One said that a rebellion of taxpayers was in the offing; Arab sponsors abroad were putting up funds for an 'alternative municipality' to which people could turn for the necessary help with maintenance in Arab districts. Some of those present scoffed, but one of Kollek's ex-advisors said privately that several projects proposed by the municipality had been turned down in the past because funds had been provided by 'outside sponsors' – the PLO or Jordan. The PLO supports by loans of up to 10,000 pounds even ordinary workmen who build their own houses and thus demonstrate the Palestinian slogan of '*saumud*' (steadfastness) – the determination to remain in their homeland. A representative of the Israeli unions asked the Arabs if they realized that should a rebellion of this kind take place, Israel might withdraw

its own services (national insurance, union protection and other benefits available to non-Israeli taxpayers).

There were other sources of discontent in east Jerusalem, the Arabs
told the Israelis. The police, using notorious criminals in the Old
City for their own information-gathering purposes, had failed to respond to repeated complaints against them. The university students
in the city would not support Kollek; they were solidly PLO. One
of Kollek's supporters promised the Arabs that One Jerusalem was
trying to work out a specific programme for their districts, that not
everything depended on Kollek. The answer was firm: 'Programmes
are useless. It's more important to fix the potholes in the road –
and straight away.' There was no evidence at this meeting, however,
that the Arabs feared a major change might be in store if Kollek
was followed by a right-wing mayor. Kollek not only symbolizes
Jerusalem so completely that many supporters abroad would only
donate to *his* re-election, and to none other; he also symbolizes Israeli
rule to the Arabs of the city. As Sabah Chevsi, present at the meeting,
said when asked about an alternative: 'But we know no one else;
Teddy Kollek is the only Israeli mayor we have had.'

Meanwhile, as Kollek's supporters and dependants worried and
argued among themselves, the Mayor brooded. Kollek had never had
confidants, and none of his colleagues really knew what was going
on in his mind. To the casual observer, he appeared to have lost
much of his famous aggression; he was almost withdrawn, absent-
minded. He showed his age for the first time. But Kollek had always
been a fighter, and he was a fighter still.

Kollek had faced the worst crisis of his career, one which had
threatened not only to destroy him personally, but to wipe out much
that he had achieved over twenty years in Jerusalem. Despite his
threats, and despite the predictions of many who claimed to know
him well, he had not resigned. Resignation would have been seen
as an admission of personal responsibility for the misdeeds, if such
they were, of colleagues and subordinates in local government, and
of inability to cope with the city's conflicts during one of the most
troubled periods since 1967. While at one time he had admitted that
he might have been guilty of errors of judgement in the administration
of the 'Teddy Fund', he now defiantly refused to wind it up. He

had always maintained that it was legitimate to use his mayoral powers in what he saw as Israel's best interests. The only real question, for Kollek, was whether he had established a consensus in the city in favour of his 'pluralist' policies, or whether, as he clearly believed, much still remained to be done, and he was the man best equipped to do it.

Above all, Kollek had not yet wrested from the government the special status, and economic help, he wanted for the city. The administrative changes proposed by investigating committees, and endorsed by the government itself in October 1986 – changes which would have given the municipality far more autonomy over city affairs – had scarcely begun to be implemented, notably in matters of education where Kollek himself had scored some considerable victories. So, on the question of whether or not he would run for another term in 1988, the messages from City Hall continued to be blurred. Some reports had it that the Mayor had definitely committed himself to running; others were doubtful. Discouraged, some of those who had rashly put themselves forward as alternative candidates – like Labour's Uzi Narkiss, the reserves general who had taken part in the battle for Jerusalem in 1967 – disappeared from view. Others whose names had been mentioned – Shlomo Hillel, the Knesset speaker, and Ezer Weizmann, like Kollek a political maverick and currently a minister without portfolio in the coalition government – prudently held their peace.

Meanwhile, One Jerusalem had organized a mass rally on 25 February, as the city's tribute to the Mayor. By Kollek's own standards, it was a modest affair; there were to be no international stars, no foreign VIPs, just a handful of local singers, and tickets sold off without fanfare, without placards, a domestic celebration rather like those surprise parties which are never wholly a surprise for their beneficiary.

Three thousand of Kollek's admirers crowded into the auditorium of the big convention hall at the entrance to the town; they included the President of the State, Chaim Herzog; the Minister of Education (and other surviving members of Ben Gurion's 'young men') Yitzhak Navon, Shlomo Hillel, many Knesset members, and a cross-section of Kollek's electorate. 'Isn't this all a bit too much?' asked Kollek, flower in buttonhole, looking round the packed auditorium. The audience loved it.

Kollek's speech was, as always, brief. The difference was that this time he was reading from a prepared text, and that – though few knew it – he had promised those around him to say nothing that would commit him to a further term. He said that he had not wanted a celebration. He saw the tribute as one to Jerusalem, and not to him personally. He had enjoyed the privilege of serving the city. He stressed, as always, the problems and challenges of his work – not his successes. He described the 'recent disturbances' in the city as 'worrying', but claimed that they had been exaggerated, and that the exaggeration disturbed him more than the events themselves.

Then Kollek came to the moment everyone had been waiting for: his future plans. 'At my age', he said, 'a man has to take stock, reconsider.' Had he the strength to go on, he asked, particularly since he was so uncertain of support from the government? He would make no commitment, he said, meanwhile. He would have to consult with his wife Tamar (by all accounts his only confidant). In any case, the Mayor concluded, there was ample time to decide – more than a year till the next elections. He thanked the audience again for coming, paid his final compliments.

Then his old trouper's instinct got the better of him. 'See you all in my next term!' he shouted, and the audience roared its approval.

Index

Index

Index

About the Author

Naomi Shepherd was born in Cardiff, brought up in London, and educated in London and at Oxford University. She has been political correspondent in Jerusalem for the *New Statesman* (1963–78), and a contributor to the *New York Times* (1974–78) and other papers in Great Britain and the United States. Her first book, *Wilfrid Israel*, a biography of a hitherto unknown figure in refugee rescue work during the Second World War, won the H.H. Wingate Prize for 1984, and was followed by *The Zealous Intruders: The Western Rediscovery of Palestine*. She is married and has three children.